A Concise

for

Macintosh System Software

ALSO AVAILABLE

A Concise Introduction
to the
Macintosh System and Finder

by
Jerry Glenwright

BERNARD BABANI (publishing) LTD
THE GRAMPIANS
SHEPHERDS BUSH ROAD
LONDON W6 7NF
ENGLAND

PLEASE NOTE

Although every care has been taken with the production of this book to ensure that any projects, designs, modifications and/or programs etc. contained herewith, operate in a correct and safe manner and also that any components specified are normally available in Great Britain, the Publishers and Author do not accept responsibility in any way for the failure, including fault in design, of any project, design, modification or program to work correctly or to cause damage to any other equipment that it may be connected to or used in conjunction with, or in respect of any other damage or injury that may be so caused, nor do the Publishers accept responsibility in any way for the failure to obtain specified components.

Notice is hereby also given that if equipment that is still under warranty is modified in any way or used or connected with home-built equipment then that warranty may be void.

© 1991 BERNARD BABANI (publishing) LTD

First Published – March 1991

British Library Cataloguing in Publication Data:
Glenwright, J.
    A concise introduction to the Macintosh system and finder
    1.   Operating systems
    I.   Title
    005.43

ISBN 0 85934 243 3

Typeset by Sixty 3 ink, Bath, Avon
Printed and Bound in Great Britain by Cox & Wyman Ltd, Reading

Preface

With its user-friendly WIMP interface, the Mac can be used productively right from the start without the need to learn complex command sequences. Beginners welcome a helping hand however, and even the experienced can't always remember the exact way to perform some much-needed function – this book will fill the gap.

A comprehensive explanation of the Macintosh pictorially-based interface coupled with clear instructions on getting the most from the machine.

Jerry Glenwright.

ABOUT THE AUTHOR:

Graduated in Computer Science and worked as a programmer and network analyst for several years before becoming Technical Editor of popular computer hobbyist magazines *New Computer Express* and *ST Format*. Edited *Atari ST User* and *Amiga Computing* and is currently working as an author and freelance journalist.

TRADEMARKS:

Apple, Apple Macintosh, Apple Lisa and Mac are registered trademarks of Apple Corporation.

IBM and IBM-PC are registered trademarks of the IBM Corporation.

MS-DOS is a registered trademark of Microsoft Corporation.

MacWrite is a trademark of the Claris Corporation.

for Pip...
...and Blue too

CONTENTS

Chapter 1

WHAT IS THE FINDER?

In the beginning, when most computers required complex and obscure command strings in order to get them to do something useful, the Xerox Corporation of America was experimenting with a new concept in computer control – a 'point and click' operating system.

Using a device known as a 'mouse' to move an on-screen 'pointer', the user was able to select programs and associated data files represented by tiny pictures ('icons') and manipulate them at will, thereby negating the need to remember commands. Although successful in that the system worked, it was never used in a commercial product by Xerox.

Soon after, Apple, then riding high with its Apple II computers, decided to produce a machine based around the 'point and click' concept. The result was the Lisa and though an excellent machine, its somewhat excessive price tag effectively locked out many would-be users. Undeterred, Apple quickly got to work on the Macintosh. The new computer had a WIMP (Windows, Icons, Mouse and Pointers) user interface known as the 'Finder', it was fast, powerful and above all, friendly. The Macintosh, or 'Mac' as it's affectionately known, was (and is) incredibly successful, spawning a large range of Macintosh machines each more powerful than the last, but each retaining compatibility throughout the range.

The popularity of the Macintosh is undoubtedly due to its use of the graphically-based Finder operating system, but what is the Finder? What can it do and how can you use it to manipulate programs, files and the like?

To understand what the Finder is and what it does, it will help to understand the interaction between the computer's hardware, its operating system and the software you want to use. A collection of silicon chips with a screen and keyboard is all very well, but unless there's a program to command this hardware, the computer has about as much 'intelligence' as the average house brick.

Do you simply buy a word processor, spreadsheet or whatever

and run it on the hardware? Not quite. Before a program can perform useful tasks, it is necessary for it to communicate with the computer, displaying characters on screen, getting key presses, producing meaningful sounds and so on. There isn't much point in re-writing these functions every time they're required and so every computer comes with its own operating system, a collection of routines which bridge the gap between users, their software and the machine.

And as well as acting as a go-between for the software and hardware, an operating system enables the user to load, save and delete files, create directories, copy disks and perform all the other mundane tasks associated with everyday computing. Unfortunately, this is where the average user encounters problems. Operating systems have many features, and many hundreds of commands in order to access those features, and beginners and experts alike find it difficult to remember complex command strings. This is where the Finder steps in.

The Finder Desktop

The Finder provides and maintains a graphic control environment known as the 'Desktop'. The Macintosh Desktop is roughly analogous to your own real-world desktop, in that it is a centre of operations containing all of the most useful items required for productivity. Figure 1 shows a typical Desktop display.

Rather than a blank screen with a prompt for you to type in the next command, the Finder Desktop displays graphical representations of files, programs, floppy and hard drives and so on. A pointer is available to enable you to select those icons. The Finder Desktop is generally known as a WIMP environment, an acronym meaning windows, icons, mouse and pointer.

Windows are framed areas of the screen used to display information. You can have more than one window on the screen and they can be made to overlap. Although several windows can be open, only one can be accessed at any one time. The window which can be accessed is described as being 'active' and is made so by selecting it with a click of the mouse. The information you

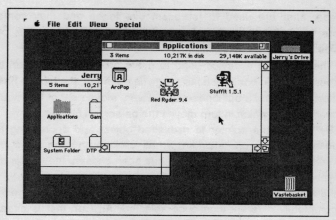

Fig 1. Finder Desktop

want to display in a window may be larger than the area available, in which case it is possible to scroll both vertically and horizontally through the information until you've seen all of it. Sometimes, you can enlarge a window to see all of the information contained within it. Windows appear by being opened and disappear after being closed. Imagine them as peep-holes into information.

Icons are tiny drawings which represent programs, documents, data files, disk drives and so on. The icon is intended to provide a pictorial 'hint' as to what the object it is representing is, a box with text and a hand with a pen might be used to represent a word processing program, a sheet of 'paper' with lines of text may represent a word processed document. Icons ensure easy recognition of the object you require. The Finder has standard icons to represent floppy disks, a wastebasket for deleting files and the like.

All Macintosh applications come with icons and many are intricate and appealing – a boon to the quick location of desired objects. Each icon has an associated line of text naming the object. The popular communications program *Red Ryder* for example displays its own unique icon together with the name *'Red Ryder'* beneath it. Figure 1 shows a selection of icons including the wastebasket, some meaningful application icons and several folder icons.

These latter are used to represent directories and may contain more 'nested' folders (imagine a collection of Russian dolls one inside another).

The mouse is a device used to move around a pointer on the screen. A plastic box which fits snugly in the hand, the mouse has a button on top and a ball underneath. Every movement of the mouse moves the ball which in turn moves the on-screen pointer.

By moving the pointer to a desired object and depressing the mouse button (an operation known as 'clicking on'), the object can be selected. To show that an item has been chosen, the Finder displays an inverse icon, that is to say in reverse video (reversing white and black). Occasionally, an application icon will change into a completely different icon once selected. An icon that is already selected is deselected by a further click of the mouse. If you click on any other item after selecting an icon, the original is deselected.

To run programs, open folders and so on, the mouse button is depressed twice in quick succession – known as 'double-clicking'. This has the effect of choosing an object and performing a relevant operation on it. Folders are opened, programs run, floppy and hard drive directories listed etc. And because the Finder is 'intelligent', and 'remembers' the applications installed on a floppy or hard disk, it is possible to click a file generated by a particular application – such as a word processed document – and have its associated application run. The data file you double clicked will be loaded into the application automatically once it's running.

To move objects around with the mouse, a process known as 'dragging' is performed. The mouse pointer is moved to a desired object and its icon clicked on. But instead of releasing the mouse button, it's held down. An outline of the icon appears, which can be dragged around the window, onto the Desktop, into the trash for deletion and so on.

Two methods exist to select multiple files with the mouse, 'shift-clicking' and 'lassoing'. Shift-clicking involves moving to and selecting one icon with the normal clicking method, while subsequent items are selected by clicking while holding down the shift key. Lassoing is the process of clicking and holding the mouse button at

4

a point adjacent to the desired items, then dragging the resultant rectangular outline around these items. When all of the icons are enclosed within the lasso, the mouse button is released, and the items are displayed in inverse video and selected. See Figure 2.

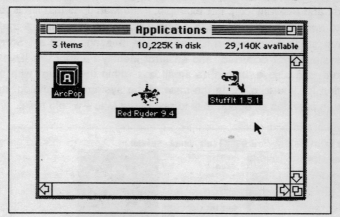

Fig 2. Highlighted Icons

Pointers come in many shapes and sizes, but there will always be a pointer available to you on the Desktop or in an application. Usually the pointer is a small arrow. This becomes a watch with moving hands when the Mac is busy and cannot respond to your commands (such as when it is accessing a disk, performing a complex reformatting action during word processing etc.).

As well as windows and icons, Finder provides a range of other items to enable you to communicate your commands to the computer. At the top of the Desktop (along the top of the screen), there is a menu bar. This contains the names of a variety of menus ranged horizontally across its width which, if clicked on and held, cause a further list of options in a box below the original menu name (see Figure 3) to pop up. If the mouse pointer is moved down the list within a menu, each option becomes highlighted in turn and these are selected by releasing the mouse button.

In order that the Finder can give warning of problems, ask for information or inform you of some unexpected happening, dialog boxes are provided (note American spelling). A box appears on-screen, overlapping whatever you're currently doing, with a message and relevant icon. For example, if the Mac finds that life is too hard and is about to crash, a dialog will appear containing a traditional 'stage' bomb with a lighted fuse, a message such as "Sorry! A system error occurred" and an error identity number like ID=15. There is a also a 'button' (a small box within the dialog) with an option for you to click. In the case of the system error dialog, the button provides an opportunity to restart the Mac – a cold reset.

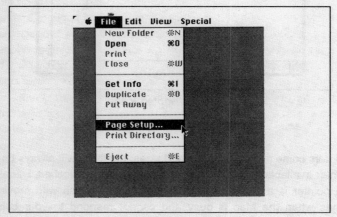

Fig 3. The File menu

Dialogs are also used when the Mac wants you to insert a disk, when you're formatting floppies, copying files and so on. The dialog box is what helps to make the Mac an extremely friendly machine to work with and the often humourous messages help to smooth your way through difficulties.

Working with windows
To make the Finder Desktop resemble the efficiency of your real desktop as closely as possible (and thereby provide its efficiency), it

is possible to change the size of windows, move disk and trash icons, drag application icons from their folders onto the Desktop for easy location etc., (a full explanation of customising the Mac Desktop is provided in Chapter 2).

Almost all windows provided by the Finder, whether they're on the Desktop or within applications, can be resized and repositioned to suit you. When a window is active, the strip at the top of the window (known as the title bar) is filled with horizontal lines. In the title bar, you can see the name of the disk you're looking at, or the name of the folder you're currently in or the name of the document you're in the process of editing. The title bar helps you to navigate your way around the Desktop and through applications. By clicking and holding the lined bar, an outline of the window appears and this can be dragged around the Desktop and the window repositioned. Release the mouse button when the outline occupies a chosen location and the window instantly appears at the new site. The reposition function is useful when there are several windows open on the Desktop and you need to view and move between them.

As with most window operations, dragging is only possible on a window which is currently active. But like most limitations in the Macintosh operating system, there is a way around this restriction. If you need to move windows without making them active, here's how to do it. Simply hold down the Command key on your keyboard, click the window you want to move (on the title bar...) and drag. The current active window remains active, and the inactive window is moved.

In the top left-hand corner of a window, at the left of the title bar there is a plain white box called the 'close box'. In order to close a window (thereby making it disappear), click on the close box. It appears to 'implode', signifying that you've clicked it then, when you release the mouse button, the window disappears. If, after clicking the close box, you move the pointer away without releasing the button, the close box clears and the window remains active. There is another way to close an active window and that is by choosing the 'close' option from the File menu on the menu bar. This is however, somewhat slower.

Clicking the close box or choosing close from the File menu will close only one window – the active window – at a time. To close every window currently open on the Desktop, hold down the Option key on your keyboard while clicking the close box of the currently active window. It will close, followed by all other open windows on the Desktop. This is extremely useful if you're becoming confused by a lot of open windows, you have run out of space for windows on the Desktop or want to shut down the system quickly.

In the top right-hand corner of a window, there is a symbol which looks like a box with another, smaller box inside it in the upper left corner. This is called the 'zoom box'. The zoom box is used to make the window you're viewing as large as possible. Clicking the zoom box produces an implosion similar to that in the close box and the window becomes as large as your screen (while leaving enough room for the trash and disk icons). Another click in the zoom box returns the window to its previous size.

In the bottom right-hand corner of a window, there is the 'size box' symbol. This looks like a small square on top of the left-hand upper corner of a larger square. Clicking the size box causes a re-sizable outline of the window to appear. The outline can be moved anywhere relative to the left corner. After releasing the size box, the window reappears at the new size.

Often windows show only a small part of some much larger document, list of files or what have you and in order that you can see the rest of the information, scroll bars are provided at the right and bottom of the window. The bottom scroll bar has arrows pointing left and right and the right scroll bar has arrows pointing up and down. In addition, each scroll bar has a scroll box. By clicking and holding the scroll bar arrows, a document can be made to scroll up or down, left or right to suit your needs. You can scroll to the top, middle or bottom of the information quickly, by clicking in the grey scroll area or by clicking and dragging the scroll box along the length of the scroll bar. Information isn't scrolled until the scroll box is released and consequently, it can be a little difficult for beginners to determine when to release the scroll box, but with practise, it is possible to become adept at precise positioning.

The amount of scrolling achieved with the scroll box is directly proportional to the size of the document being scrolled. Moving the scroll box two or three centimetres when viewing a small document therefore, may move from the very top to the very bottom. The same amount of movement with a large document however, might only succeed in scrolling the document a few lines – practise is the only key to accurate and efficient positioning.

Editing the Desktop

The Macintosh Desktop is designed to be personalised. Unlike other computer systems, you can name floppy and hard disk drives, folders and other objects on the system with anything you want – including spaces – up to 32 characters in length (well, almost anything. In fact, if you use a colon when naming an object, it will automatically be changed to a hyphen). You can also drag application icons from their folders onto the Desktop and position them anywhere.

To edit the name of an object, click its icon then move the pointer to the text beneath it. The pointer will become an I-beam, and then any part of the name (or all of it, using a double-click...) can be highlighted and changed. You can rename any icon, including those of the drives, in this way. A full description of personalising your system is in Chapter 2.

Chapter 2

DESKTOP MENUS AND ACCESSORIES

In the previous chapter, we touched briefly on the menu bar. Now it's time to learn about what you can find there. The menus, from left to right are:

Apple File Edit View Special Colour

Each menu is selected by clicking its name ('Colour' only appears if you're using a Macintosh II with a colour monitor) and provides access to features and functions of the operating system not found elsewhere. Click and hold a menu name to make it pop up. To choose a function from a menu, drag the pointer (keeping the mouse button held down) until the required function is displayed in inverse video. By releasing the mouse button, the action is performed. The functions available from a menu are described as being 'under' that menu.

The first menu on the menu bar is the Apple menu. Under the Apple, you can get information about the Finder and access to desk accessories (known as 'DAs'). Here is what's available from the standard Apple menu (that is, before any extra DAs have been added to the system):

About the Finder...
Alarm Clock
Calculator
Chooser
Control Panel
Key Caps
Scrapbook

When a function is followed by an ellipsis (...) this means that choosing that function causes a dialog box to appear on screen. 'About the Finder...' for example, produces a dialog box bearing the names of the Finder's authors and its version number. If a function doesn't have an ellipsis, then its action will usually be performed immediately. Back to the All about Finder... option. There's a figure showing the total amount of RAM memory installed in your Macintosh and a memory graph depicting how the available memory is shared between the System and Finder. Earlier versions of the Finder don't have a memory graph.

Next on the menu bar is the File menu. Under File you'll find:

New Folder
Open
Print
Close
Get Info
Duplicate
Put Away
Page Setup...
Print Directory...
Eject

Many of the functions including New Folder, Duplicate and Eject can be selected using a combination of keys ('hot keys'). The New Folder function for example, can be chosen from the File menu or executed by pressing Command-N (the command key is at the left of the keyboard and has a 'clover leaf' symbol). **New Folder** creates a new folder in the currently active window with the name 'empty folder'. Folders are the equivalent of directories on other computers. They behave just like cardboard folders that you have at home or school. Folders are used to store programs and data – or more folders – and you can create and name them at will. A newly-created folder is displayed in inverse video – it is active – and to rename it, just type in the new name. Press return, and there'll be a newly-named, folder which you can open, fill with applications or within which you can create more folders.

Open performs the same action as a double-click. If you click a folder or drive icon then select Open, the folder opens and its window appears on the Desktop. Clicking an application icon and selecting Open causes the application to run. If you open a document, its associated application will run and the document is loaded ready for use. You cannot open a document without the application which created it being on a disk currently recognised by the system (a floppy or the hard disk). If you try, a dialog appears to tell you that the application is busy or missing.

Open is useful if you want to work on more than one document at a time. You may, for example, have several related word processed files all of which require some extra editing. By shift-clicking each in turn then Opening, the application which created them is opened and each document loaded into memory. You can then move between and edit each of them. Open can be chosen by pressing Command-O.

Print enables you to send documents from the Desktop to a printer without the need to open the application which created them. Printing in this way mimics printing from within an application so that if you're printing documents created using Claris's *MacWrite* word processor, you will be presented with a print dialog which looks just like the one you would receive from within the program (see Figure 4). You can choose several documents to print but they

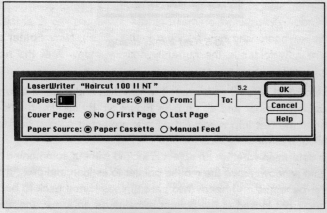

Fig 4. Claris's MacWrite print dialog

13

must all be generated by the same application and you cannot print any document whose application is not on a disk currently recognised by the system. To print, click the item(s) you want and select Print. A dialog box appears. Modify the options required such as orientation, scale and so on, then click the OK button. Your documents are reproduced on the printer. See Chapter 6 for a full explanation of printing documents.

Close has the same effect as clicking the close box in a window. If you want to ensure a precious file can't be thrown into the wastebasket or deleted, click it then choose **Get Info**. This causes a dia-

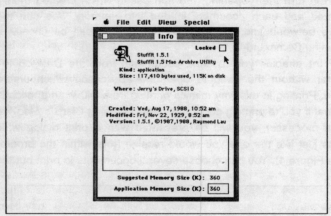

Fig 5. Get Info... dialog

log to appear which contains lots of useful information about the item including when it was created, which disk and folder it belongs to, version number and so on (see Figure 5). By clicking the 'lock' button in the Get Info window, the file is protected against accidental deletion or modification.

To determine whether an object is locked without summoning the Get Info window, move the mouse pointer to its icon and click. If the pointer becomes an I-beam (two parentheses joined back to back), the file is not locked, if the pointer remains as an arrow, the file is locked. A box at the bottom of the Get Info window is provided for notes about the file or program. You can type whatever you want into this box using standard cut and paste operations to edit the information. Any text that you type here is stored in a hidden information file known as the Desktop file. This stores system information about programs, files and folders and where these objects are stored, and is extremely important to the operation of the Finder. At least one computer virus attacks the Desktop information file and there are various operations which can be performed on it. For more information, see Chapter 3.

Duplicate enables a copy of any file to be made. Click the icon of the file you want to duplicate (or select several items to duplicate by shift-clicking or lassoing) then choose Duplicate from the menu or press Command-D. An exact copy of the object, including its icon, is created and deposited on the same disk in the current folder. The newly-created object is called 'Copy of nnnnn' where nnnnn is the name of the original. You can edit and rename the duplicate in the normal way (as described in Chapter 1). If the name of the original combined with the phrase 'Copy of' is greater than 32 characters (the normal maximum length for a file name), you'll be regaled with a dialog informing you of the fact and requiring you to type in a new name of suitable length.

One of the great advantages of the Finder Desktop is that you can drag the icons of your applications from their folders onto it, where they can be seen and accessed with ease. There may come a time however (such as when the Desktop has become cluttered) that you want to put them back from whence they came. It can be very difficult to remember just where the icons should go. This is where **Put Away** comes into its own. Any item on the Desktop can be returned instantly to its original folder by clicking it, then selecting Put Away. And it doesn't stop there. If you've dragged an item to the wastebasket for deletion and have relented and decided to keep it, simply clicking and choosing Put Away, the reprieved object is restored to its rightful place. The Put Away function is very useful if you regularly access a large number of files.

Page Setup works hand in hand with **Print Directory**. These two functions enable you to print a directory listing of the current window. Using Page Setup, the orientation, page size and various other formatting functions are selected then, when Print Directory is chosen, a directory is sent to your printer.

In order for the Finder to work efficiently and with maximum speed, the Macintosh operating system does not update floppy disks until the last possible moment – before launching an application, ejecting a disk, when you've flushed out the wastebasket and so on. This does mean however, that if you were to remove the floppy disk from a Mac before the system had a chance to update it, serious loss or corruption of data could result.

To ensure that you can't remove disks, the Mac floppy drive does not have the disk eject button of many other computers. In fact there is, mechanical means to remove a disk. So how do you retrieve a disk? Several methods exist, and **Eject** (or Command-E) from the menu bar is one of them. Eject will first update, then 'spit out' a selected floppy disk. After being ejected, a disk's icon and applications icons are dimmed to show that they're no longer available.

Next on the menu bar is the Edit menu. This provides cut, paste and other functions to enable you to edit objects on the Desktop. Here's what you'll find under the Edit menu:

Undo
Cut
Copy
Paste
Clear
Select All
Show Clipboard

Undo or Command-Z, enables you to reverse the last action performed – think of it as a board game's 'go back one space' card. Imagine you are working with a favourite word processor when you accidentally delete all the text you've just typed in. Choose Undo and it's instantly returned. The properties of the Undo command vary from application to application, so you need to experiment to find out what it can do for you within any particular application. On the Desktop, you will find that it is invaluable when you make disastrous mistakes deleting text from a Get Info window, cutting the contents of the clipboard and so on. When you need it, you *really* need it!

Cut, **Copy** and **Paste** (or Command-X, Command-C and Command-V respectively) are text operations which enable you to manipulate selected amounts of text quickly and easily. Cut removes text (but makes a copy on the Clipboard – a temporary system storage area, more soon), Copy duplicates selected text, placing the duplicate on the Clipboard while leaving the original intact. Paste inserts the contents of the clipboard at a desired point. **Clear** removes selected text without making a copy in the Clipboard and **Select All** selects all the text in the current, active text window. The selected text can be manipulated by the other functions. Select All is also useful on the Desktop for choosing the entire contents of a window when you want to make a copy or delete them. The function is also useful when you want to choose almost all of the items in a window. Rather than shift-clicking or lassoing everything, use Select All (or type Command-A), then shift-click the items you don't want. The rest can be dragged around the Desktop as normal.

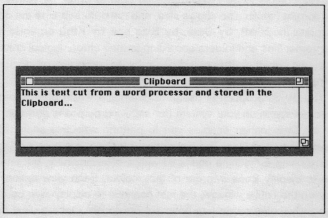

Fig 6. The Clipboard

The Clipboard is a temporary storage area which enables you to cut, store and paste text from different sources on the system. **Show Clipboard** causes a window to appear, enabling you to view the contents of the Clipboard (see Figure 6).

The View menu allows you to choose the way you want to display and organise objects in windows on the Desktop. The View menu provides the following options:

by Small Icon
by Icon
by Name
by Date
by Size
by Kind
by Colour (if you're using a machine equipped for colour)

Each of the View options enables you to order and display window contents to suit your needs. If a particular window is stuffed with programs and documents for example, then it might be a good idea to display their icons using the '**by Small Icon**' option. **by Icon** causes objects to be displayed using normal icons, **by Name** in a text format (which also shows size, and the date and time the object was last modified), **by Date**, **by Size** and **by Kind** organise your programs, files and folders according to their chronological creation, size and whether the object is a folder, program or document respectively.

The **by Size** option is useful to determine which objects require the most space on your system (for archiving purposes perhaps) and the **by Date** option enables you to perform selective searches on recently updated files. The last option, **by Colour** is only available if you're using a machine equipped with a colour monitor, but enables you to display icons in order of their colour. Each view option acts only on the active window, the rest continue to display their contents using whichever mode has been set previously. Once a view mode has been selected a tick appears to the left of its menu entry.

The final menu on the menu bar is the Special menu. This is where the system-related functions can be found. Here is what you'll find there:

Clean Up Window (or 'Selection' or 'Desktop')
Empty Wastebasket
Erase Disk
Set Startup...
Restart
Shut Down

The Finder Desktop is supremely flexible. You can arrange icons anywhere within a window thus allowing great freedom. You can gather together program icons, recently edited files and so on, to enable you to select them easily at the next session. Unfortunately, there is a price to pay for flexibility. Windows become cluttered very easily and unless you are the type of computer user who arranges icons in regimented rows, you'll probably end up with a mass of jumbled objects in any given window. This situation can be counter-productive as your eyes scan this way and that in an attempt to locate a program or document.

Fortunately, the Finder has a solution: **Clean Up Window**. Select this function, and the icons in the active window move into orderly spacings as if by some unseen hand. Alternatively, with a group of icons selected, when you pull down the Special menu **Clean Up Selection** is available. This function slots chosen icons into available spaces on an invisible grid. When the Desktop is free of windows and there are no icons selected, the Clean Up option is **Clean Up Desktop**, enabling you to order any icons dragged onto the Desktop into regular spaces.

In order to operate at maximum speed, the Finder does not update floppy or hard disks until the last possible moment such as before a disk is ejected. This has the advantage of allowing you to drag a deleted item back from the wastebasket if you change your mind. But because deleted items are not actually removed from the disk until it is ejected, you won't gain the space made free by deletion. **Empty Wastebasket** enables you to flush deleted items from the wastebasket, thereby freeing space on your disks. Issue the Empty Wastebasket command, and deleted items are completely removed.

Erase Disk is described in Chapter 4.

Set Startup... allows you to run an application automatically when you start the Macintosh (see Chapter 3). After selecting the function, a dialog appears (see Figure 7) from which you can choose a program. Unless you are running MultiFinder (see Chapter 9), it is only possible to run one application on startup.

Restart is a quick way to perform a 'warm reset', that is, restarting the Macintosh without actually turning the power off then back on. Applications are closed (after first saving) and any floppy disks are ejected. Restart is useful if you want to to start the Mac from a new startup disk (see Chapter 3).

As stated earlier, the Finder does not perform disk updates until the last moment. This means that unlike other computers, it is not a good idea to simply switch off the machine when you've finished. Before power off, you should always use the **Shut Down** function. This ejects inserted disks (first saving information), flushes the wastebasket, and generally leaves the system neat and tidy. After issuing the Shut Down command, the screen goes black and a dialog appears with a message telling you it is safe to switch off the Mac. There is a restart button if you change your mind and decide to continue.

Desk accessories

To simulate the flexibility of your real desktop as closely as possible, the Finder Desktop provides a selection of 'desk accessories' or 'DAs'. These are pop-up utility programs which provide help when you need it most. Imagine you're at a desk writing a letter to your bank manager, and need to calculate budget figures. You'd simply reach across to a drawer and pull out a calculator. DAs provide precisely this type of assistance. And because they are stored on disk and not brought into memory until needed, you can use large DAs without wasting valuable RAM memory.

Available from the Apple menu, DAs can be accessed from within any application, so you could use a word processor and select a calculator from the Apple menu, or a clock or a scrapbook etc. And the added advantage of the desk accessories provided by the Finder is that the information from a DA can be copied and pasted into any other DA or into an application. You can copy and paste the time from the clock into a spreadsheet, a result from the calculator into a word processed document and so on.

The standard system comes with six basic desk accessories: Alarm Clock, Calculator, Chooser, Control Panel, Key Caps and Scrapbook.

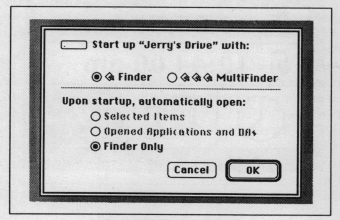

Fig 7. Set Startup... dialog

The **Alarm Clock** has a digital read-out with an AM/PM indicator. When selected, the clock is displayed in 'compact' form – that is, a single line with the time in hours, minutes and seconds, but to the right of the time read-out there is a 'lever'. Click this, and two more panels are displayed (see Figure 8). These are used to set the time, date and alarm.

Let's say you want to change the date. Click the calendar icon in the middle of the bottom panel. Move the pointer to the middle

panel, where it will become a set of cross-hairs. Now click each part
of the date in turn. A button appears showing up and down arrows.
Click either to advance or retard the date. Both time and alarm are
set in the same way, but to switch the alarm function on, click the
lever to the left of the alarm time in the middle panel. The alarm
clock icon in the bottom panel changes to show lines radiating out
from the bells. When the alarm goes off, you'll hear a sound (or the
menu bar will blink depending on whether system sound is turned
on. See Control Panel entry in this section).

Fig 8. The Alarm Clock

Ignore the alarm, and the Apple symbol on the menu bar flashes
constantly until you finally turn it off. To do that, select the clock,
move the lever until the extra panels drop down, select the alarm
icon, then click the alarm on/off button. To copy and paste the time
and date into another application, open the clock, then use the
Command-C/Command-V sequence (or their equivalents from the
menu bar) to cut and paste. When the clock is on screen, its display
is automatically selected, so there is no need to highlight the read-
out.

The **Calculator** behaves exactly like any other four function
device. To use it, select it from the Apple menu then click the num-

bers in its display, or use the Mac's keyboard (everything corresponds exactly). You can paste results from the calculator into other applications using the Command-C/Command-V key strokes.

The **Chooser** is described in Chapter 6.

The **Control Panel** enables you to change system parameters such as volume, screen background pattern, mouse speed and so on quickly and easily. In early versions of Finder, the control panel was a simple affair offering the bare minimum of control. Later versions of Finder have a 'modular' control panel. That is to say, the control panel does not have a fixed number of parameters, but incorporates any control panel documents stored in the System Folder when the control panel DA is loaded. A modular control panel can be used by both Apple and third party suppliers to provide a huge range of extra system control options (one of the most popular third party control panel documents is *SoundMaster*, which allows system events such as restart, disk eject and so on, to be accompanied by some very effective digitised sound samples). Any changes that you make using control panel are remembered by the Mac even after you have switched the machine off. Figure 9 shows the control panel.

When the control panel is selected, the 'General' icon is high-

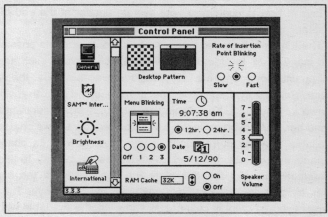

Fig 9. The Control Panel

23

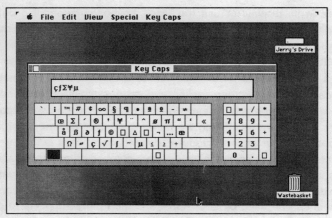

Fig 10. Key Caps

lighted and all of the general system features such as rate of insertion point and menu blinking, time and date (the time and date can
be set from the control panel as well as the clock) are displayed. To
alter one of the parameters, click its icon on the left of the control
panel. The right side then changes to provide the features associated with that parameter. To see all of the icons available in the control panel, use the scroll bar just to the right of the parameter icons.
Details of how to customise your system appear at the end of this
chapter.

The Finder is provided with a range of fonts and it is possible to
add many more. In order to locate certain characters, such as special punctuation marks etc., **Key Caps** is available under the Apple
menu. Select Key Caps, and you are presented with the window
shown in Figure 10. Key Caps also insert an extra menu into the
menu bar. The keyboard in the Key Caps window shows characters
available with the current font. If you press a key, its character
appears in the horizontal aperture above the 'keyboard'. To find the
character you want (or to explore the possibilities of the current
font), try pressing the Option, Command and Shift keys. The Key
Caps keyboard display changes to show what is available with the
Shift and special keys depressed. To change fonts, pull down the

24

Key Caps menu from the menu bar and choose a new font.

The **Scrapbook** is used as your personal store for pictures and text. You might, for example, have a favourite illustration that you created using a paint package and that you like to include with letters and other documents. This can be stored in the Scrapbook and pasted into any application. Or you might want to cut and paste between DAs, and applications – the Scrapbook acts as a temporary store between them (see Figure 11). To use the Scrapbook, cut or copy some text or a graphic from an application or DA using the Edit menu or Command-X/Command-C keystrokes, choose Scrapbook from the Apple menu and when its window appears, paste in the selected image or text.

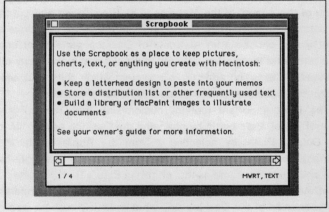

Fig 11. The Scrapbook

A horizontal scroll bar below the Scrapbook's image window allows you to scroll through the Scrapbook's pages. As each piece of text or picture passes, it is automatically selected, so to copy an item from the Scrapbook, use the scroll bar until it appears in the window, choose Copy from the Edit menu, close the Scrapbook, then paste the item into your chosen location. A counter at the left of the screen displays the amount of items stored in the Scrapbook (and which item you are currently viewing...).

25

Once an item is pasted into the Scrapbook, it remains there until removed with a Cut command from the Edit menu. The contents of the Scrapbook are stored as a disk file in the System Folder known as 'Scrapbook File'. A Scrapbook will only be recognised by the system if it is called 'Scrapbook File' (note capitals and spaces). This means that you can create a range of Scrapbook files to suit different needs simply by renaming them 'Scrap – letterheads', 'Scrap pictures' and so on and storing them in a folder outside the system folder. When you want to use a new Scrapbook file, rename it Scrapbook File and move it to the System Folder (after removing the original, or it will be overwritten).

Personalising your system with Control Panel

Much of the appeal of the Mac lies in its friendliness and potential for personalising. You can change the names of the disk drive and other icons, choose from a variety of Desktop patterns or create your own, alter the blinking rate of the menus and make many other changes. All of which adds up to a system which suits your needs. Computing becomes almost a pleasure rather than a chore.

The most important tool for customising the Desktop is the Control Panel. Let's begin by changing the Desktop pattern. Invoke the Control Panel by selecting it from the Apple menu. If the 'General' icon isn't highlighted, click on it, so that the right-hand side of the panel resembles that shown in Figure 9.

At the top of the window, in the middle, you'll see a miniature representation of the Desktop and what looks like a chess board to the left of it. The chess board is a magnified image of the Desktop (each black and white square is a pixel). The best way to examine the possibilities of the Desktop pattern is to click on the checked board. Where there are white squares a click will render them black and vice-versa. Immediately you click on the checked board, the pattern on the miniature Desktop will change. Alter several pixels, then click on the Desktop. The real Desktop behind the Control Panel will instantly change to whatever pattern you've created on the miniature.

When you have tired of creating patterns, click the right arrow on the menu bar of the miniature Desktop. A previously created pattern appears and its magnified image is displayed on the checked board. Scroll forward through the pre-prepared patterns using the right arrow, move back via the left arrow. There are some amazing patterns to choose from, but you might find that good old grey is the best of all!

The Mac is equipped with a variety of squeaks and buzzes which act as warnings, and attention grabbers. Some users like these sounds, others do not – and that is where the volume control comes into its own. In the right most corner of the General control panel screen there's a sliding volume control. To change the sound level, simple click and drag the volume slider to the desired level.

The other parameters are all self-explanatory and the best advice is to experiment. You can't damage the machine in any way, so feel free to try out different settings.

Chapter 3

PREPARING YOUR SYSTEM

The Macintosh will normally be sold to you with the System and Finder software already installed by your dealer. If you buy the Mac and its hard drive separately however, then it will probably be necessary to prepare the system for use yourself. This is not difficult, and can be achieved by anyone with a little application.

In order to boot up (i.e. become available for use. 'Boot up' comes from the adage 'pulling yourself up by your bootstraps'), parts of the Mac System and Finder must be loaded into the machine's memory. This operation is performed automatically (after switching on the power), with a disk known as the 'Startup Disk'. The Startup disk can be a floppy or hard drive as long as there is a valid version of the System and Finder stored on it (usually in a special folder called the 'System Folder'). Current versions of the System and Finder attach a special icon to any folder with the name 'System Folder' (see Figure 12). To create a disk with which to start the Macintosh, simply open a new folder and call it System Folder, then copy a System and Finder into it.

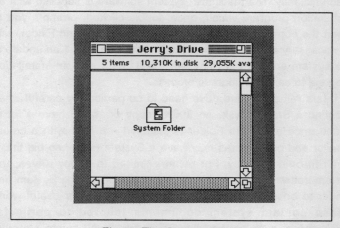

Fig 12. The System Folder

29

Well, that will start your Mac, but there's a little more to the System Folder than meets the eye. Finder is responsible for the Desktop, menu bar and so on and System performs all of the system-level operations such as disk drive control, but there are a lot of extra system functions performed without your knowledge, and the objects associated with these functions are stored in the System Folder too. Documents determining keyboard layout (whether American or International) and control panel options (see Chapter 2), the Clipboard and Scrapbook files, printer drivers, fonts, system utility programs and a good many other items are stored in the System Folder.

You must try never to have more than one System Folder on a Startup disk. System and Finder are complex control programs which can become confused if there are two or more System Folders on your hard drive. Almost all commercial applications come with a System Folder on their disks which you may inadvertently copy when installing the application. To ensure that only one System and Finder exists on your hard drive, check with a utility such as Find File (see Chapter 7).

Fortunately, for the most part, you don't need to know what is in the System Folder or alter its contents directly, in order to use the Mac efficiently. The Macintosh system software is supplied with an installation program which, once double-clicked, prompts you to insert the correct disk and installs a valid System and Finder, with all necessary extras, onto your hard drive. Similarly, if an update of the system software is released, it will come with an installation program to ease the upgrade process.

Users without a hard drive need to be particularly careful when creating a Startup disk. An 800K floppy does not have a lot of space once a System Folder is installed – a Mac with a colour monitor and other extras may have a System Folder so big that it won't fit onto a floppy. For owners limited to floppy drives, the system software comes with miniature versions of the System and Finder to ensure that enough space is left over for useful work. These contain system documents tailored to particular Macintoshes, such as the Plus, SE and II. If you create a startup disk containing a mini System and Finder, you won't be able to start other Mac models.

Before installing system software, make a backup of the system disks (see Chapter 4 if you don't know how to copy a disk). Insert the System Tools floppy disk into your Mac, then locate and double-click the operating system installation program called Installer. A 'welcome' dialog appears, click OK, then the installer-proper dialog appears (see Figure 13). Select the disk on which you want to install the System and Finder using the Switch Disk button, then click Install. The installation process begins. You will be prompted at intervals for the disks necessary to install the operating system. After a little while, the process is completed and if all went well, a dialog appears to inform you of the fact. Click the Quit button on

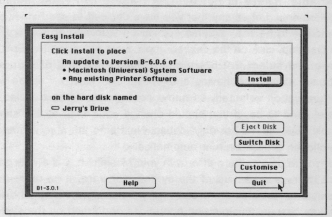

Fig 13. The Installer

this dialog and you are returned to the Desktop. The System and Finder are now installed and you can start to use the Mac properly.

Once the system is installed, you can decide on what happens at startup, whether you should use Finder or MultiFinder, choose an application to run automatically and so on. MultiFinder is a version of the Finder which enables the Mac to 'multi-task'. That is to say, enables the machine to run several programs at the same time. You could, for instance, use a desktop publishing package, a text manipulation tool to create text effects and a paint program to illustrate your publication. Rather than quitting the DTP program then running the paint package, a simple click of the mouse places the DTP program into the background and brings the paint package into the foreground. The process is analogous to the operation of windows on the Desktop. You can choose any program to become active in the same way that you choose any window without having to close the current, active window, and you can switch between them with a simple click. A full description of MultiFinder is in Chapter 9.

If you elect to use Finder upon startup, only one application can be chosen to run automatically – with MultiFinder, several are available. There is however, a trade-off in RAM memory requirements. Let us say that you have decided to use Finder and would like to have a favourite application launched on startup. On the Desktop, click on the desired application, pull down the Special menu and select Set Startup... A dialog like that of Figure 7 appears, except that having entered the Set Startup... option with an application selected, its name now appears where 'selected items' used to be. If you should change your mind at this stage, simply click the 'Finder only' option. Next time the Mac is started, the chosen application runs automatically.

If you're using a hard drive with your Macintosh, it is a very good idea to have a backup of the system software. It is, of course, possible to re-install the system software using the original disks, but any changes/customising operations performed on the system will be lost. You would also need to re-install any DAs or extra fonts that were installed into the System file (a full explanation of installing DAs and fonts appears in Chapter 7). If you're using a lot of DAs and fonts and the System Folder contains a lot of extra files, it may be too large to copy to a floppy disk. If this is the case, then don't bother to copy all of the extra items in the System Folder. If possible, keep a copy of the System and Finder on a floppy in a safe place, so that you can recover easily should the Macintosh crash for any reason.

Chapter 4

WORKING WITH FILES

Today's floppy and hard disk drive systems can store huge amounts of programs and data. A floppy disk, initialised for use on one side only can store 400K – enough for several hundred pages of text. A double-sided floppy disk holds twice that amount, and a hard drive described as 'small', has an enormous capacity of 20 megabytes. Use a hard drive-based system for several months, and you would soon find it a sprawling mass of lost applications and data without, that is, the help of folders. These are directly analogous to cardboard folders stored inside the filing cabinet. The hard or floppy disk is a filing cabinet and the disk's folders, the electronic equivalent of their cardboard namesakes. You can create as many folders as you wish (subject to the size of the disk), assign them names to suit your needs, then fill them full of files.

The Macintosh organises its file structure in hierarchical fashion. At the top most level there is a root directory which is what you see after double-clicking a disk drive icon. The root directory holds a number of files and folders. Double-click a folder, and its contents – more files and folders – are displayed. Each time you open a folder, you are moving one level down, and away from, the root directory. Folders within folders are described as being 'nested'. Figure 14 shows how the root directory, folders and files are organised. Note how the structure resembles a family tree. On the Desktop, clicking a window's close box closes the window and moves back up the structure by one level. The window which then becomes active is the 'parent' of the one you just closed.

Folders are especially useful when using the Macintosh with a hard drive. A folder can be assigned to every type of object stored on the system. Applications in one folder, letters to your bank manager in another, household accounts in a third and so on. Alternatively, with a large number of applications, a folder can be assigned to each so that, for example, your word processor, spreadsheet, paint program and database all have individual

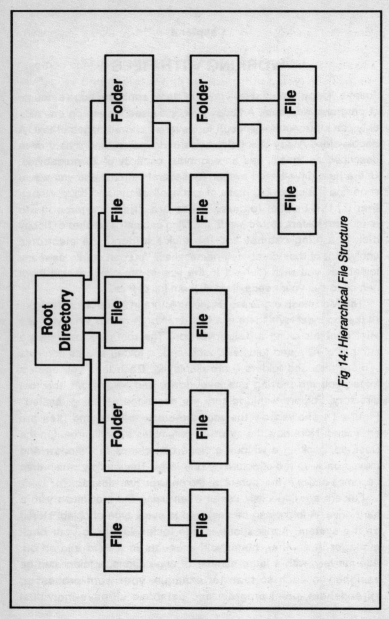

Fig 14: Hierarchical File Structure

folders. Data generated by an application is then stored in another folder within that of the application.

To create a folder, select New Folder from the File menu or press Command-N (you can only open a new folder with an active window on the Desktop). A folder icon appears, displayed in inverse video with the name 'Empty Folder' (see Figure 15). Rename it by typing the new name. The empty folder is already selected so you don't have to move the pointer to it or highlight the existing name. Once named, the folder can be opened and used to store objects. You can create a new folder in the root directory of a

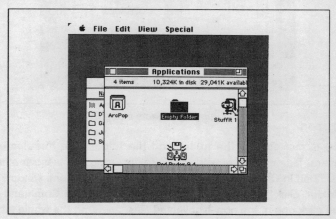

Fig 15. A newly-created folder

disk or within another folder using the menu or Command-N method. It is possible to nest lots of folders but in practise, most users find three of four nested folders to be sufficient for their needs. More than this, and you will spend more time than is necessary searching for items stored deep within the structure, thereby negating the effectiveness of nested folders.

Folders can be renamed at any time by clicking on them. The pointer becomes an I-beam with which you can select part or all of the folder's name, by clicking and dragging or by double-clicking. Then simply type in the new name.

To move a file into a folder, click and drag the file over the folder icon until it becomes selected (the folder icon is displayed in inverse video. See Figure 16). Release the mouse button, the file

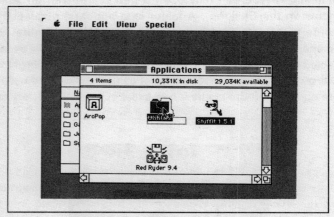

Fig 16. Dragging objects into a folder

icon is moved into the folder and the folder icon deselected. Several files can be moved into a folder using the lasso method described in Chapter 2. To move all of the files from one window to a folder, click 'Select All' in the Edit menu or press Command-A, then click one of the now-highlighted files, and drag the whole lot to their new destination.

Renaming files

You will often need to rename files with similar names, rename files to show they are no longer current or needed, or simply to change names that were originally conceived during a silly moment. You can rename any file except those which have been locked using the Get Info... dialog (see Chapter 2).

Click on the file's icon. The pointer becomes an I-beam. Now simply type in the new name. If you only want to change part of the name, click and drag the mouse pointer over the characters you want to change.

Getting Information

Associated with any object stored on the system is information describing its size, date of creation and so on. To get information about an item, click on it, then select Get Info... (or press Command-I) from the File menu. A dialog appears and in the case of folders, you are presented with the size, date of creation, last date of modification and the number of files the folder contains (see Figure 17. A program's Get Info... dialog appears in Chapter 2). An application information dialog also shows the version number if it is available, whether or not the application is locked, and its suggested memory size (the amount of RAM assigned to it by the Finder, when running).

Copying files

Files are not duplicated when moved between folders. Moving a file merely removes it from its original location, installing it elsewhere. To make a copy of a file, click on it, then select Duplicate from the File menu. Alternatively, press Command-D. A dialog box appears informing you that the Finder is making a copy of the chosen file. The duplicate has the name of the original preceded with 'Copy of'. Once created, it remains selected, so you can rename it simply

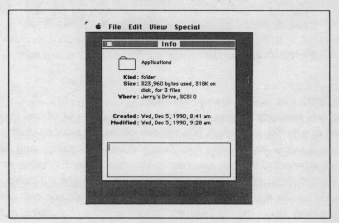

Fig 17. Get Info... for a folder

by typing the new name. If your attempt to duplicate a file would result in the duplicate having a name larger than 32 characters, a dialog appears prompting you to enter a smaller name (see Figure 18). The duplicate is created in the current active window. You can then move it anywhere on the system.

Files are duplicated when copied between drives (floppy to floppy and floppy to hard drives). A dialog appears telling you how many files are left to copy. There's a moving graph indicating how far the copy has proceeded and a line of text above it detailing which files the Finder is currently reading and writing.

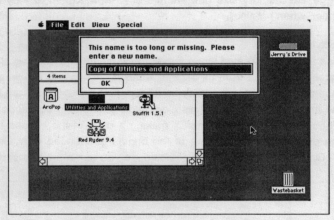

Fig 18. Duplicate file names are limited to 32 characters

Copying one floppy disk to another

Several methods exist to copy the complete contents of one floppy disk to another and which you choose depends upon whether you have a single floppy drive, two floppy drives or a floppy and hard drive connected to your Macintosh. You can't copy the contents of an 800K floppy disk to a 400K floppy disk – there isn't enough space on the 400K disk. Always write-protect the source disk using the sliding tab in the top left-hand corner of the disk (looking at the back of the disk with the metal sliding window facing down). The disk is write protected when you can see through the hole left by moving the sliding tab.

1. **With one floppy drive.** Insert the destination disk into the Macintosh (the destination disk is the floppy which is to receive the copied files), make sure it's highlighted, then select Eject (or press Command-E) from the File menu. If the destination disk is new, you will need to initialise it before continuing with the disk copy (see Chapter 8 for an explanation of how to initialise floppies). The disk is ejected from the Mac, but its icon remains, dimmed, on the Desktop. Now insert the source disk (i.e. the disk from which the files are being copied), and click and drag its icon onto the dimmed icon of the destination disk. A dialog appears informing you of the specifications of the copy you're about to initiate (see Figure 19). Click OK, and the disk copy begins. If there are a number of files/folders to be copied, you may need to swap disks several times (sometimes dozens of times) before everything is copied. When complete, you will have a destination disk which is an exact copy of the source disk.

2. **With two floppy drives.** Insert the destination disk into one drive

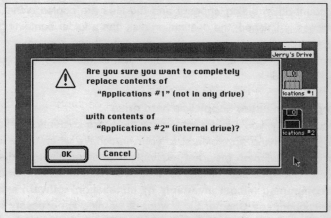

Fig 19. A copy dialog

and the source disk into the other. It doesn't matter whether the destination disk is in the second internal or external drive. Click and drag the source disk over the destination disk, then release the mouse button. A dialog appears to tell you that you are about to delete the entire contents of the destination disk. Click OK, and the copy begins. A 'count-down' dialog keeps you posted on the progress of the copy. When the process is finished, the destination disk is an exact copy of the source disk.

3. **With one floppy and a hard drive.** You can make an exact copy of a floppy drive without the need for lots of disk swaps even if you have only one floppy – as long as you have a hard drive too. Insert the source disk and if it isn't selected, click on it. Drag the source disk icon to the hard drive icon and release the mouse button. A dialog appears telling you that the two disks are of different types and a folder, with the same name as the source disk, will be created on the hard drive. Click OK, the folder is created, and the contents of the source disk are deposited in it.

Eject the source disk by dragging its icon to the wastebasket and insert the destination disk. If this is new, a dialog appears offering to initialise the disk. Accept the offer. Now drag the folder containing the source disk contents from the hard drive to the destination disk. A count-down dialog appears and the files are copied. When the process is finished, the destination disk has a folder containing the items from the source disk. You can drag these items out of the folder and discard it. The destination disk is then an exact copy of the source disk.

Copying an entire floppy to a hard drive
Occasionally, you might want to copy the entire contents of a floppy disk, preserving any folders, to your hard drive when there is no proper installation program available – after receiving a disk of useful public domain utilities for instance. (Commercial software is accompanied almost invariably by installation software – for a description, see Chapter 5). A word of warning is necessary here. Take care when copying applications disks wholesale to the hard

drive. Applications disks usually have a System and Finder which is also copied to the hard drive. Two Systems and Finders can severely confuse the Macintosh and cause it to crash. If you find that you have inadvertently copied another System and Finder, simply drag them to the wastebasket.

1. Copying to the root directory of the hard drive. Insert the source disk and drag its icon to the hard drive's icon. A dialog appears informing you that the two disks are of different types and a folder will be created on the hard drive using the name of the source disk. Click OK, the folder is created and the contents of the source disk copied to the folder in the root directory of the hard drive.

2. Copying to an existing folder on the hard drive. Insert the source disk, then open windows on the hard drive until the folder you want to copy to is displayed. Double-click the source disk to open a directory window, then pull down the Edit menu and choose Select All or simply press Command-A. All of the files and folders contained on the source disk are selected. Click one, and drag the whole lot to the folder you want to copy to. A count-down dialog appears to inform you of progress.

3. Copying to a new folder on the hard drive. Perhaps you want to copy lots of new utilities, games or the like to your hard drive but don't have an existing folder suitable. Or you may want to try them out before committing them to existing folders where they will end up being kept at a cost of space. The solution is to create a new folder and copy the disk to that. After deciding what to keep, you can drag the folder to the wastebasket.

Insert the source disk, then click and open the hard drive icon. Select New Folder from the File menu or press Command-N. A new folder appears in the hard drive's directory window with the name Empty Folder. This folder is already selected so to rename it, simply type in the new name. Now double-click the source disk and press Command-A to select the entire contents. Click one item and drag all of the objects to the new folder. A count-down dialog appears to keep you posted of the copy progress.

Protecting files

You should protect valuable documents and applications against accidental deletion, and there are two ways to do this. The first simply involves sliding the write-protect tab in the top left-hand corner of a floppy disk (looking at the disk fom the back with the metal sliding window pointing down) so that you can see through the window which the tab covers. The disk is then physically write-protected and files cannot be deleted from it. If you try, a dialog appears to tell you the disk is locked.

The second method involves selecting the file to be protected, then summoning the Get Info... dialog. This has a 'lock' button in the top right-hand corner which, once clicked, locks the file against renaming and deletion.

Deleting files and folders

Sooner or later you will need to delete an unused file to reclaim space, rid the system of junk documents or trash empty folders. Finder provides a very friendly wastebasket with which to delete unwanted items. To delete an object simply drag it to the wastebasket, release the mouse button and its icon disappears inside. When the wastebasket contains deleted files and folders, its sides swell out (see Figure 20). Once emptied, the wastebasket regains its slimline proportions (early versions of the System and Finder don't have a swelling wastebasket).

The friendly feature of the wastebasket is that you can open it (by double-clicking) and reclaim a deleted file! To maximise system efficiency, Finder does not empty the wastebasket until the last moment before ejecting the disk which contained the file, or before launching an application. The wastebasket is also emptied by selecting Empty Wastebasket from the Special menu.

You cannot delete any item which has been locked using the locking option in the Get Info... dialog. Dragging a locked object to the wastebasket results in the icon flipping across the screen to its

Fig 20. Swollen Wastebasket

original location. It is technically impossible to delete a locked file without first unlocking it, but like most technical impossibilities on the Mac, the operation is possible if you know how. Simply press the Option key when dragging the icon to the wastebasket, and it is deleted without fuss.

Chapter 5

WORKING WITH APPLICATIONS

Applications is the word used to describe programs that you run on the Macintosh. Word processors, spreadsheets, painting programs and databases, are all examples. Applications are used to create letters and other documents, calculate budgets, design publications and perform all of the other useful tasks for which your Mac is perfectly suited.

Applications is also used to describe utility programs which alter the Mac's system parameters, drive printers, repair and restore floppy disks, kill viruses and so on. (Some of the system utility programs are described in Chapter 7).

The Macintosh provides a set of useful routines known collectively as the Toolbox, in order that applications programmers write software which conforms to standard conventions. This is to ensure that applications on the Macintosh all make use of the point-and-click operating system and provide an intuitive method of control. Occasionally, you will discover applications (usually public domain utilities) which don't conform to the Mac's 'way of doing things', but on the whole, the bare bones of one application look very much like another.

Installing applications

After buying an application, you don't simply copy all of the files from the master program disks to the Mac's hard drive. Most applications come with a series of installation programs and procedures to enable the software to mould itself to your hardware. If you are installing the software onto a hard drive, it will be necessary to create new folders and often, there are naming conventions for these folders which can't be altered. The software also needs to know which printer you have, how much memory, the size of the screen, whether you have a colour system and so on.

Most of the installation process takes place without your knowledge. You won't have to tell the program that your machine has a screen larger than nine inches or more memory than 1Mb, the software runs its own checks and determines the hardware specifications. Usually, installation is a simple matter of double-clicking an installation program and following the on-screen prompts. The Macintosh system software itself, comes with an installation program similar to that of some commercial software (see Figure 13 in Chapter 3).

Running an application

There are several ways to run an application and the one you choose depends upon whether you wish to open a new document or continue editing one created previously. The first method is to locate the icon of the application you want to run and double-click it. The Desktop clears to present a blank screen with a title bar containing the name of the application you are running. Within a few seconds, the title bar changes to show the options which will be available from the within the application, and the blank Desktop becomes whatever screen the application presents.

As an alternative to double-clicking, you can click once on the application's icon to highlight it, then select Open from the File menu. The Desktop clears as before and the application runs. Both the double-clicking and the click/open method launch an application without taking into account documents previously created using the application. With the application running, you wil be invited to begin on a new document. If you want to edit existing work, then you have to close the new document, and open the old one.

If however, there is already an existing document which you want to edit, then rather than double-clicking or opening the application, find the document you want to work with and double-click or open that. The application runs as before except this time, the document you double-clicked appears on screen ready for editing.

Here's a tip. Many applications allow you to have more than one document in memory at the same time and to switch between them to edit. If there are several documents that you want to work on, shift-click or lasso them so that they're all highlighted, then double-click any one of them. The application which created the documents runs, and all are loaded into memory. You can then switch between them at will. Obviously, you can only shift-click and load documents emanating from the same application, but the shortcut is an extremely useful and timesaving one.

Finder within applications

One of the most appealing features of the Mac, and its biggest design criterion, is that all applications – should – conform to the same WIMP principles of operation, thereby enabling users of the machine to quickly become familiar with computing. And once one application has been learned, others, being similar, can quickly be assimilated too.

This continuation of the WIMP interface throughout different applications means that there are 'standard' Mac operations which you can expect from all applications running under the Finder. Almost all applications have a menu bar, providing such options as File, Edit and the like. You will also have access to the Apple menu at all times so that you can use DAs, alter system parameters using the control panel and so on. Almost all applications have editing windows similar to those on the Desktop, with slider scroll bars, window resize and close boxes and a title bar.

Edit keys such as those for cut, copy and paste (Command-X, Command-C and Command-V respectively) should all remain the same across applications. To create a new document within an application, select New from the File menu or press Command-N. A document is opened with the temporary name 'Unititled'. If you have opened an application with a new, blank document but wish to close it and continue editing an existing document, click the window close box in the top, left-hand corner (just below the apple of the Apple menu). The screen clears to present a blank screen. Pull down the File menu and select Open or press Command-O. A dia-log appears presenting you with a list of files in the current folder (i.e. that containing the application's icon. See Figure 21). If the file that you want to open is listed, double-click it or click on it to high-light it, then click the Open button. The document is opened and appears on screen. If the file isn't listed but the folder in which it is

47

stored is listed, double-click that. The list changes to show the contents of that folder and you can then select the desired file.

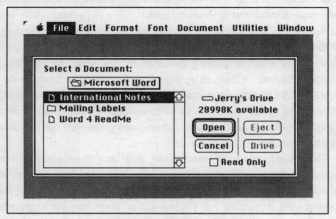

Fig 21. File selector dialog

If you can't see the file you want to open (because it is in a different folder), click and hold the folder indicator button which appears above the list of files. A list of the parent folders of the current, displayed folder drops down. You can drag a selector bar down this list of folders and releasing the mouse button selects the currently highlighted folder. If you should change your mind about opening a document, click the cancel button to quit the operation.

Most applications use the mouse to good effect too. When editing text in a word processor for example, click and drag the mouse to highlight specific blocks of text to cut, copy, count or spell check. Most word processors enable you to select an entire word by double-clicking it and some enable you to highlight a whole line by treble clicking or moving the I-beam (the pointer is always an I-beam while you are editing text) to the beginning of a line where it becomes an arrow. Clicking once then selects the line.

Cut, copy and paste is available from the Edit menu or via key commands to enable you to cut images and text from a document and place them at the current marker (the marker is a blinking line which marks your position within a file, not the arrow or I-beam pointer) position.

You can cut, copy and paste text and pictures between different applications too. Choose the desired item to copy and paste using the mouse to select it and Command-C keystroke to make a copy (or Command-X to cut it out of the original altogether). Leave the application by selecting Quit (usually from the File menu) or pressing Command-Q. You will be asked if you want to save the clipboard. Click OK. Back on the Desktop double-click the application you want to paste to, or double-click an existing file. When the program is running, pressing Command-V will paste whatever you cut into the clipboard into the new document.

A very useful command available with almost all applications is Undo. This is the equivalent of the board game's 'go back one space' and allows you to reverse the operation of the last command. If, for example, you've just cut a large amount of text that you would rather have back in place, select Undo from the Edit menu or press Command-Z. The cut text will reappear instantly. You should determine whether the application you are using is equipped with an Undo function before relying on it to reverse an unintentional command however, because the function is not always available.

Saving documents

To save a document you have just edited, select Save from the File menu or press Command-S. You can also use the Command-S key combination at any time during the editing process to save your work so far. The Save function saves your document with the name it had prior to the edit. If the file you wish to save is a new, un-named document, a dialog, similar to the standard item selector dialog, appears after issuing the Save command, prompting you to name the document and choose a folder in which to save it (see Figure 22). A blinking marker flashes in the text window waiting to receive the new name. Simply type in the file's name. If it's larger than the space allowed in the name box, it will scroll to the left as you type. Click and drag the folder button as normal to choose a location in which to save the new file, then click the save button. You can quit the operation at any time by clicking the 'cancel' button. Clicking the 'drive' button enables you to save the file to a disk other than the current disk.

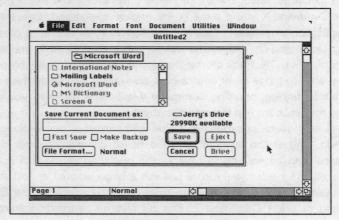

Fig 22. Naming a new file

The Finder and applications do not normally create backup copies of exisiting files when replacing them with updated versions. If you want to create a backup, there are several methods to achieve this all involving the Save As... function from the File menu. The first is to Save As... with the same name but to a different folder. Here's an example. You have just edited the manuscript of your latest novel, but you're not sure whether to keep the changes. Select Save As... from the File menu, then click the folder button on the file selector. Choose a new folder in which to save the updated MS, then click the save button.

You can use this method to save to a different disk too. If the existing file is located on the hard drive, insert a floppy disk and click the 'drive' button on the file selector after issuing the Save As... command. The drive icon next to the folder button changes to show a floppy and the file lister window shows the files on the root directory of the floppy. Click the save button to save the file.

Leaving an application

You must never simply switch off the Mac in order to leave an application. All applications have a 'quit' option, usually available under the File menu (or by pressing Command-Q), to enable you to return to the Desktop. Using the quit function ensures that the application shuts down properly, saving any information unsaved during the recent edit. If you switch off the machine before quitting an application, data will almost certainly be lost. You may even find that the Mac cannot reboot properly when next you switch on, because the Finder is confused about what happened before you switched off.

After selecting quit, you will be prompted to save any unsaved data, then the application will stop running and you will be returned to the Desktop. You can then run another application if desired.

Chapter 6

PRINTING YOUR DOCUMENTS

The Mac is equipped with two serial ports, one designated as a modem port and the other as a printer port. Both can be used to drive printers, but usually, the printer port itself is fine. There is no inherent printer driver in the System or Finder and so to print, you must first install printer drivers into the System Folder. Fortunately, a number of such drivers accompany the Mac's operating system disks and so printing is a straightforward process. If, that is, you are using a standard Apple printer such as an ImageWriter or LaserWriter. If your printer is an Epson, Mannesman Tally, Panasonic and so on, then you will need to find a suitable printer driver. An Epson driver is available which will cope with most of the devices from other manufacturers which have an Epson emulation mode, and there are other drivers available from the public domain.

Installing a printer driver

If you bought your Mac with the System and Finder pre-installed, then it is a safe bet that the system 'Installer' program was used which automatically copies all printer drivers on the system disks into the System Folder. Check to see if drivers are installed by double-clicking the System Folder and scanning for files such as 'LaserWriter', 'ImageWriter' and the like. If you can't find them, simply drag them from your system disks into the System Folder.

The correct driver for your printer must be installed using the Chooser (see Chapter 2 for a description of the Chooser) before printing can take place. Pull down the Apple menu and select Chooser. A dialog like that of Figure 23 appears on screen. The box on the top, left-hand side of the Chooser dialog shows which printer drivers are available from the System Folder. By clicking the appropriate printer driver for your printer, the box immediately to the right of the printer driver box, the device box, displays all the devices which can be driven by the printer driver you selected, currently attached to the system. In most cases of course, only one printer

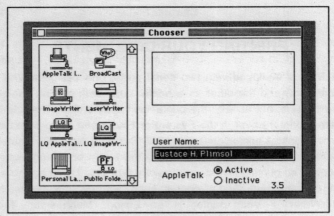

Fig 23. The Chooser

will be on view. In large offices however, a number of printers may be available. The final step is to click the name of the printer in that box. If the printer you want to access is a LaserWriter (but not a LaserWriter IIsc), then you will also need to click the 'Active' button of the AppleTalk option below the device window. LaserWriter laser printers operate by making use of AppleTalk, the Mac's built-in local area network.

Preparing to print using Page Setup...

There is still one step before you can print, and that is to tell the Mac how you would like the document to be printed – its orientation, size, whether you want to use printing enhancements and so on. To do this, select Page Setup... from the File menu. A dialog appears bearing options for the type of printer you selected using the Chooser.

If your Mac has an ImageWriter dot matrix printer attached, then a Page Setup... dialog (see Figure 24) has the following options: you can select a paper size ranging from US Letter (a kind of 'wide' A4), US Legal and A4 Letter, to International Fanfold and Computer Paper. There is also a column of 'check boxes' which display or remove a cross when clicked. The check boxes come under the

54

title 'Special Effects' and allow you to adjust the size of the printed output and skip continuous stationery perforations.

A Page Setup... dialog for the LaserWriter (see Figure 25) enables you to choose a paper size including US Letter, A4 Letter, Tabloid and so on. You can reduce or enlarge the printed output by any factor up to 100 per cent and switch between vertical and horizontal paper orientation. The check boxes under Printer Effects allow you to sacrifice quality of printing to speed and vice versa. Obviously, an important letter or final draft of a magazine must be printed in the finest quality possible. When printing a proof draft however, speed is more important than quality. The best advice is to experiment with the printer effects until you have decided on the best possible selections to suit your needs.

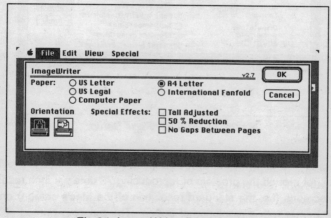

Fig 24. ImageWriter Page Setup...

Down the far right of the dialog is a series of buttons the first of which, 'OK', saves the current page setup, including any changes you made. Next there's a 'cancel' button which quits the dialog preserving the previous page setup. The 'Options' button provides a further set of page enhancements. After clicking Options, you can elect to print an inverted screen (i.e. print a negative), increase the size of the printed area (at the expense of memory and usable fonts), flip the printed image or choose to have an unlimited supply of downloadable fonts. The latter option means that your printer can reproduce fonts not already installed, by downloading the information necessary to reproduce the font from the Mac. Don't select unlimited downloadable fonts if the LaserWriter attached to your Mac has only 1Mb of RAM or the printing operation will be impaired.

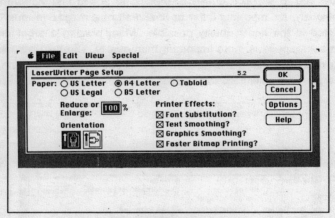

Fig 25. LaserWriter Page Setup...

There is also an option known as 'bitmap alignment'. This is provided to get around the problem of reproducing 72 dots per inch resolution screens (i.e. the standard resolution of the Mac's screen) on a laser printer with a resolution of 300dpi. The output is printed at 96 per cent of the original size (96 per cent of 300dpi is 288dpi – divisible by 72) significantly improving the quality of the results.

Those are the standard Page Setup... dialogs. Most applications however, provide extensions to Page Setup... to enable you to extract a variety of extra application-specific features from your printer. Microsoft's popular word processing program Word for example, provides a couple of extra buttons in its extended ImageWriter Page Setup... dialog, including a 'Document...' button. Clicking this button produces another dialog enabling you to determine where to print footnotes, alter margin and gutter settings and so on.

Under normal circumstances, the best setup for a LaserWriter page is A4 Letter, vertical orientation with faster bitmap printing switched on. And for an ImageWriter page, A4 Letter and vertical orientation.

Printing a document

After installing printer drivers and choosing a page setup, you are ready to print one or more documents. Normally, you will want to print from within an application, but the Mac also provides a printing option that you can use while on the Desktop, thereby eliminating the need to launch the application before printing.

If you are editing a document and decide to print, the usual procedure is to select Print... from the File menu (or press Command-P). A print dialog appears enabling you to choose how many copies you want to print, select a source of paper and, if you are using an ImageWriter, the method of feeding paper into the printer and whether you want to print in draft, faster or best quality mode (see Figure 26). Click OK after choosing the options you want, a dialog appears informing that printing is taking place and your document is printed.

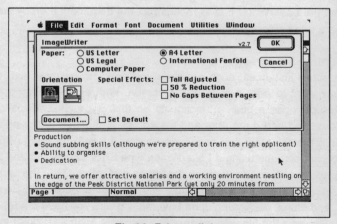

Fig 26. Print... dialog

You can print one or more documents while on the Desktop too. Shift-click or lasso the desired items, then select Print from the File menu. The Print dialog appears, click the options you want and click OK. The documents are printed. The only restrictions to Desktop printing are that multiple files must be generated by the same application and reside in the same folder.

If you should change your mind about printing a document, you can cancel the print operation by typing Command-. (i.e. Command and a full stop). You may need to do this more than once to win the Mac's attention. If the Mac refuses to recognise your demands and you are using an ImageWriter, simply turn it off (the printer ...) and after a few moments, the Mac realises that there is no longer a printer responding to its instructions and stops trying to print.

If you are using a LaserWriter, and there is a possibility that you might want to print more than one copy of a document, always use the 'Copies:' box rather than printing one copy, returning to edit mode or the Desktop, then printing again. The biggest chore for the LaserWriter (and consequently the one which consumes most time) is to 'construct' a document in memory before it is printed. Once constructed however, you can print several copies in a small amount of time. Reselecting the print function each time, means that the LaserWriter has to reconstruct the document thereby wasting a large amount of time.

Printing the screen

In some instances, such as when you need to illustrate text, you may want to print a copy of the screen. With an ImageWriter, the Mac provides a built-in function to do this. Type Shift, Caps-lock, Command and 4 together and the screen is dumped to the printer. Unfortunately, this key sequence only works with an ImageWriter. To print screens using a LaserWriter, type Shift, Command and 3 to 'grab' and save a copy of the screen as a MacPaint file. The screen grab appears in the root directory with the name 'Screen 0', Screen 1' and so on, depending upon how many grabs you have made.

Rename the file with a sensible alternative such as 'Book Figure

1', then print it from the Desktop as normal. The author has used the screen grabbing method to illustrate this book without problems.

Printing a directory

Often, when you are searching for a particular file, or trying to organise a collection of utilities, DAs and the like on disk, it would be very helpful to be able to print a directory listing of the current window (which could be the root directory of your disk or any of its folders), so that you have a paper copy you can refer to. Finder provides such a directory printing function.

To print a directory, display and make active, the desired directory window. Use the View menu to arrange the directory's files and folders in the order you require (see Chapter 2), then select Print Directory... from the File menu. A print dialog appears, click the options you want, then click OK (or hit return. Highlighted – default – buttons can be selected by pressing return). The directory listing is printed.

Chapter 7

SYSTEM UTILITIES

The Macintosh System and Finder are complex pieces of software which remove much of the drudgery from operating a personal computer. There is no need to remember obscure command strings in order to operate the Mac, simply point with the mouse, click, and your desired function is performed. To achieve this degree of sophistication however, a great many individual programs are required to work together to create the overall effect. Much of these software modules are 'invisible' to the average user, that is, you need know nothing about them to receive their benefits. But sooner or later, you will want to install a new typeface or desk accessory, find a 'lost' file, repair a damaged floppy or read the contents of an MS-DOS formatted IBM-PC disk that you've brought home from school, college or your place of work. To perform all of these functions and more, the Macintosh is acompanied by a series of utilities which you can run as needed.

Font/DA Mover

Just like your real-world desktop, the Mac's electronic equivalent provides access to a series of Desktop Accessories (DAs) such as calculators, calenders, notebooks and so on (see Chapter 2 for a full description of the standard DAs). Although these DAs are usually stored on the startup disk, you can't add more accessories simply by placing more of them on the startup disk. DAs must be installed into the System file before they can be used. That is, the DA's code is physically appended to the System file. It then appears under the Apple menu.

The Mac is accompanied by several standard DAs, such as an alarm clock and a calculator, but there are many third-party programmers and software houses providing DAs to perform a variety of tasks. You could, for example, install a communications DA, a miniature word processor or spreadsheet, games and many others.

Fonts, too, can be installed into the System file so that you can include dozens of different typefaces in your word processed or desktop published documents. The System has several built-in fonts, but many suppliers offer others.

To install or remove standard and third-party DAs and typefaces, the Mac is supplied with Font/DA Mover. Double-click Font/DA Mover and you are presented with a dialog containing two file selector windows and a sprinkling of buttons (see Figure 27). Two indicators at the top of the dialog show whether you are viewing Desktop accessories or fonts. The left-hand file list window shows the fonts or DAs currently installed into the System file. The right-hand file list shows the fonts or DAs available for installation from the chosen disk and folder. Between the file list windows there are

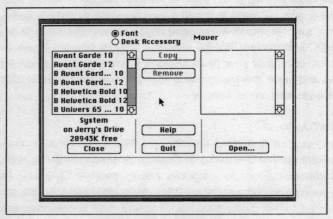

Fig 27. Font/DA Mover

four buttons to install and remove fonts and DAs, summon help or quit Font/DA mover. Below each file list window there is a button to open and close sources of fonts and DAs. At the very bottom of the dialog, below the dotted line, there is a message area.

The underlying priciple behind Font/DA Mover is that you must select one or more files from a file list window before you can install or remove anything. There are four basic scenarios: installing a DA, removing a DA, installing a font and removing a font.

Installing a DA

Double-click the Font/DA Mover to launch it. A dialog appears showing the fonts currently installed into the System file in the left-hand file list window. Click the Desk Accessory indicator at the top of the dialog to show the currently installed DAs. (Here's a tip. The Font/DA Mover defaults to showing installed fonts when launched. To manipulate DAs, you have to wait until the program has determined the installed fonts and displayed them, click the DA indicator, then wait until the System's DAs are determined and displayed. The whole process can take a very long time if you are using a lot of fonts and DAs. To force Font/DA Mover to default to DAs when launched, hold down the Option key when you double click Font/DA Mover's icon.)

Click the Open... button under the empty right-hand list window. A standard file selector appears. Choose the drive and folder where the desired DA is and select it. The Copy button is displayed in black accompanied by chevrons which point to the left-hand list window. Simply click the Copy button, and the DA is installed. Click Quit and pull down the Apple menu. The DA you have just installed is now available.

Removing a DA

Double click the Font/DA Mover icon while holding down the Option key. This will force the program to default to displaying installed DAs. A dialog appears. Use the slider bars of the left-hand file list to display the DA you want to remove from the system. When the desired DA hoves into view, click on it (to remove several DAs at once, shift-click them). Once the item to be removed is highighted, click on the Remove button. An alert box will ask whether you really want to remove the selected item. Click OK if you wish to proceed with the operation. The DA is removed. Click Quit to return to the Desktop.

Installing a font

Double-click the Font/DA Mover icon. You are presented with a dialog displaying, in the left-hand file list window, a list of the currently installed fonts. Click the Open... button beneath the empty right-hand file list window. A standard file selector appears from which you can choose the source of the fonts you wish to install. Click or shift-click the desired fonts. At the bottom of the Font/DA Mover dialog, in the message area, an example phrase (the quick brown fox...) is displayed in the chosen typeface so that you can see exactly what you have selected. If you shift-clicked several fonts however, the message area remains empty.

The previously 'greyed-out' Copy button is displayed in black. Click Copy and the chosen fonts are installed. Click Quit to return to the Desktop. Now select Restart from the Special menu. You cannot make use of any new fonts, until the Macintosh has been rebooted. When the Mac displays the Desktop after restarting, the newly-installed fonts are available.

Removing a font

Double click the Font/DA Mover icon. You are presented with a dialog displaying a list of the installed fonts in the left-hand file list window. Select from the file list the fonts you would like to remove. If you chose one font at a time, it will be displayed in the message area at the bottom of the Font/DA Mover dialog. Click the Remove button and the font is removed. Click the Quit button to return to the Desktop. You cannot make use of RAM freed by removing fonts from the System file until the Mac is rebooted. Select Restart from the Special menu. When the Mac restarts, the fonts are gone and the space they occupied is available for use.

Find File

The Macintosh file system is organised in hierarchical fashion similar to the branches of a tree. This enables you to make efficient use of a large amount of backing storage, by creating logically nested folders in which to store your files. The disadvantage of this system however, is that you can easiy 'lose' an application, utility or document – even an entire folder! Small hard drives such as the 20Mb devices can store many hundreds, sometimes thousands, of objects and a file which isn't used often can easily become misplaced. To overcome the problem of lost files, a DA called Find File is supplied with the Macintosh, which can locate any object, anywhere on a hard or floppy disk within a few moments.

Before you can use Find File, it must be installed using Font/DA Mover (see DA installation instructions at the beginning of this Chapter). Once installed, select the utility by highlighting it from the Apple menu. A dialog appears like that shown in Figure 28. To make a search, select the drive you wish to search by clicking the icon or name in the top left-hand corner of the dialog.

Type part or all of the item's name into the 'Search for' phrase box. Don't worry about using capital letters in the right place, Find File is insensitive to capitals. To the right of the phrase box, there are two icons. One is a hand inside a polygon and means 'stop' (i.e.

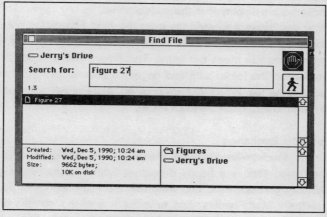

Fig 28. Find File

stop searching). The other shows a person running and means 'start searching'. After typing in the search phrase, click the running person. Find File searches the selected drive for an object with a name matching that typed into the phrase box.

If a match is made, and Find File has determined the location of the object, it appears in the middle, previously empty panel. Now click on the object in that panel, and its creation and last modification dates and size appear in the bottom left-hand panel, and its location in the bottom right-hand panel.

Find File continues to search for other matches even after one has been discovered, but you can stop it by clicking the hand icon. If no match (or no other matches...) are found, a beep is sounded, the highlighted icon changes from the running person to the hand and a flashing text indicator reappears in the phrase box ready for you to type in another phrase. With a large hard drive, the search may take some time, but by selecting Find File from the Apple menu while using an application, you can set it searching, then click the application's window to make it active (i.e. click outside the Find File dialog). Find File will continue to search in the 'background' while you work. A beep sounds when it has finished searching. Reselect Find File from the Apple menu, and any matches the utility discovered are displayed in the middle panel.

You can move a located file from the Find File dialog onto the Desktop by selecting Move to Desktop (or pressing Command-M) from the Find File menu bar entry. This means that you don't have to remember the folder path and negotiate several layers of folders to access the file. When you are finished, use Put Away... from the File menu to return the file to its folder.

Apple File Exchange

All new Macintoshes (except the Plus) are equipped with the SuperDrive. This is a floppy disk drive built into the Mac's case which can initialise, read and write IBM-PC initialised disks as well as ordinary Mac floppies. And to make use of the abilities of the SuperDrive, the Macintosh is supplied with Apple File Exchange ('AFE'), a utility which converts files to and from PC format and initialises (known as 'formatting' on the IBM-PC) floppies.

Why should you want to read and write PC disks? IBM's personal computer has been on the market for a number of years and is extremely popular in industry, where it outnumbers other microcomputers by a large factor. Sooner or later, you will need to transfer some text, a picture, spreadsheet file or similar between your Mac and a PC at work, college or school.

Apple File Exchange consists of the program itself, and several translator files kept in a folder called Apple File Exchange, on one of the Utility disks supplied with the Mac. To use the program, copy the folder from the Utility disk into a suitable position on your hard drive, or run AFE from the Utility disk (or a back up). Apple File Exchange is launched by double-clicking its icon.

Once running, the program presents a similar screen to that of Find File described elsewhere in this chapter. Two file list windows, accompanied by a variety of buttons and a menu bar complete the screen (see Figure 29). Apple File Exchange is a complex piece of software whose capabilities are many, varied and unfortunately, outside the scope of this concise text, but the program's main abilities consist of initialising, reading and writing PC disks. Here's how to perform those tasks.

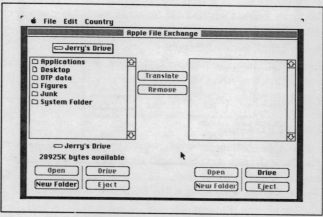

Fig 29. Apple File Exchange

Initialising a floppy for use by the Mac and IBM-PC

Double click the Apple File Exchange icon. The left-hand file list window shows the contents of the Desktop's current active window. Insert a new blank floppy disk into the internal drive. An alert box appears to tell you that AFE can't read the disk and prompts you to initialise it (see Figure 30). Click MS-DOS (MS-DOS is the PC's

67

operating system) and the 720K button, then click 'Initialise'. The disk is initialised as an IBM-PC floppy disk.

After initialising, you are prompted for a name for the disk. MS-DOS restricts file and disk names to eight characters followed by an optional full stop and three further characters known as the 'exten-der'. Spaces and leading numbers are not valid characters for names. For example, 'PROGRAMS.DTP', 'LETTERS.TXT' and 'MYDISK' are valid names, 'NAMETOOLONG.DTP', 'HAS SOME SPACES.TXT' and '123 WORKFILES' are not. After naming the disk, the naming dialog disappears and the disk's name appears below the right-hand file list window. The right-hand file list remains blank (there is, as yet, nothing on the disk).

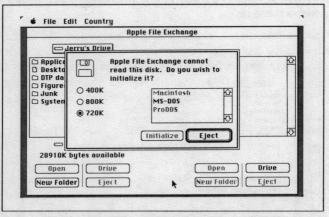

Fig 30. Initialising a 'MS-DOS' disk using AFE

Copying Mac files to an MS-DOS (or AFE-initialised) disk

Start Apple File Exchange by clicking the program's icon. When AFE is running, insert the MS-DOS (or AFE-initialised) floppy disk into the SuperDrive. The left-hand file list window shows the contents of the current active window on the Desktop, and the right-hand file list shows the files present on the MS-DOS floppy. Select the file(s) you want to transfer by clicking or shift-clicking – use the Drive button and the pop-up folder levels menu above the file list windows to choose the location of the desired files.

After selecting files, the Translate button is displayed in black accompanied by chevrons pointing to the right-hand file display. Check that there is enough space on the destination MS-DOS disk by comparing the 'bytes selected' figure show beneath the Translate and Remove buttons, with the 'bytes available' figure beneath the file list window of the disk to which you are transferring. If the size of the selected files exceeds the amount of free space on the destination disk, you can deselect files by clicking them a second time or free space on the destination disk, by clicking or shift-clicking files which can be deleted, then clicking the Remove button. When all is well, click the Translate button, a dialog with moving graph shows the status of the translation, and the files are moved to the destination, MS-DOS disk.

Files bearing names larger than those allowed by MS-DOS, are automaticaly shortened to conform to the latter's naming conventions by Apple File Exchange. If the destination disk contains files bearing the same names as the files you are attempting to transfer, a dialog appears prompting you to rename them.

Copying MS-DOS (or AFE-initialised) disk files to the Mac

This process is the reverse of copying Macintosh fies to an MS-DOS disk. Double-click Apple File Exchange and insert the MS-DOS or AFE-initialised disk. Select a destination for the files using the Open, Drive and New Folder buttons beneath the left-hand file list window (i.e. the file list of the Mac's drive), click the files you want to transfer from the right-hand file list, then click Translate. The files are translated and copied to the Mac.

Disk First Aid

The advent of the floppy disk brought new levels of integrity for electronically stored data. Unlike magnetic tape which was used extensively with minicomputers of the 1970s, the floppy disk (and particularly the 3.5 inch variety used with the Macintosh and certain other machines) provided a relatively safe and convenient storage medium with which to back up and transport programs and data.

Unfortunately, this safety is relative, and the floppy, as with all other forms of magnetic storage, is subject to corruption by heat, condensation, and electro-magnetic radiation from televisions, telephones, monitors and so on. Hard drives too, although more sophisticated and reliable than floppy disks, are nonetheless delicate devices, which a knock or mains power surge can damage seemingly beyond repair.

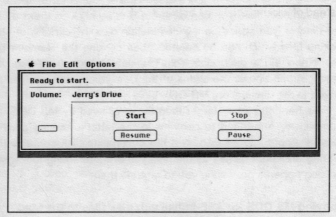

Fig 31. Disk First Aid

The first step in combating loss of data, is to ensure that you have several copies of valuable files on other floppies, and to store them in a safe place (such as a purpose made disk box). But however diligent they are, most users, at some time in their computing endeavours, will suffer the failure of a disk for which you have no copy.

Fortunately, the Macintosh system software is supplied with a utility program designed to breath life back into dead disks. Disk First Aid scans the magnetically recorded data on the surface of a disk containing a hierarchical filing system – 800K floppies and hard drives – to discover what is there and what is salvageable. Disk First Aid rebuilds damaged data structures, recreating your files. Figure 31 shows the Disk First Aid screen.

Examining and repairing floppy disks with Disk First Aid

Unless your Mac is equipped with two floppy drives, Disk First Aid must be installed on the hard drive. To do this, simply drag the program from the Utility disk supplied with the Macintosh System and Finder to a suitable location on your hard drive. Double click the program's icon. A dialog appears from which you can select a drive to examine and repair. Use the Drive and Eject buttons until the name of the drive appears in the dialog (you can press the tab key instead of clicking the Drive button if you wish).

Pull down the Options menu and select Repair Automatically. Disk First Aid requires no input from you other than a consent to continue. As you have already set the program in motion, it is assumed that you wish to continue with the examination and subsequent repair. Selecting Repair Automatically, supresses the 'consent' dialogs and speeds the process. Now click the Start button.

After the disk has been examined, you'll be regaled with a message such as "Finished. No repair necessary", or a message informing you that a successful repair was achieved. If the "Unable to verify status of disk" message appears, the disk is beyond redemption. All you can do is to reinitialise it. Return to the Desktop by choosing Quit from the File menu.

Examining and repairing hard drives with Disk First Aid

Start the Macintosh with the Disk First Aid floppy in the internal floppy drive. This ensures that the Macintosh recognises the Disk First Aid floppy as a startup disk. Disk First Aid is run automatically. Select the hard drive using the Drive button (or tab key) from the volume selection dialog presented by Disk First Aid. Pull down the Options menu from the menu bar and select Repair Automatically to supress 'consent' dialogs. Click the Start button.

If all is well and Disk First Aid is successful, a message to that effect will appear on screen within a little while. If you should receive the "Unable to verify status of disk" message however, Disk First Aid is unable to repair the hard drive and cannot retrieve your files and data. In that unfortunate situation, try contacting your dealer for an alternative suggestion. There are several third-party suppliers of hard drive repair utilities which may be successful where Disk First Aid failed. Do NOT reinitialise the hard drive at this stage, unless you have an extensive collection of back ups. It may still be possible to restore the drive to working order or retrieve the files.

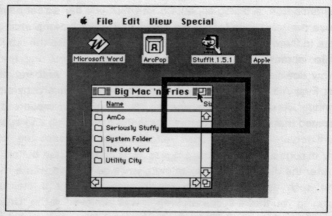

Fig 32. Using CloseView

CloseView

The 'compact' Mac's diminutive nine inch screen can be difficult to read for those users who wear spectacles, and even the monitors of the larger Macs become increasingly difficult to focus on after lengthy periods. To alleviate the problem, the Mac is accompanied by CloseView, a magnifying utility which can be moved around the screen and which presents a magnified view of whatever it covers. CloseView is also useful for users with good eyesight who wish to examine the contents of the screen in more detail such as when working with a design or paint program.

To use CloseView, copy it from the System Folder Additions folder on Utilities disk 2, into the System Folder of your Mac. Restart the machine and CloseView is automatically installed. Although installed, CloseView must be switched on before it can be used. To do that, type Option-Command-O. A rectangular outline appears on screen. You can move this rectangle by moving the mouse pointer or, if you are editing a document within an application, the rectangle moves with the blinking insertion point. To magnify the portion of the screen bounded by the rectangle, type Option-Command-X. The screen is filled with a magnified version of whatever was within the rectangle (see Figure 32). To see more of the screen, simply move the mouse pointer in the direction of the screen portion you want to view.

To increase magnification type Option-Command and the up arrow key, and to decrease it, Option-Command and the down arrow key. You can switch off magnification completely, by typing Option-Command-X again whereupon the normal screen returns accompanied by the rectangular outline.

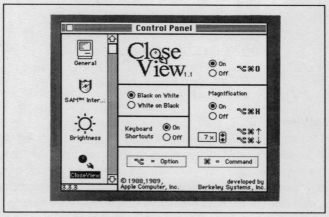

Fig 33. CloseView's Control Panel

All of the features and more can also be accessed from CloseView's entry in the Control Panel. Pull down the Apple menu and select the Control Panel (see Chapter 2 for an explanation of using the Control Panel). Use the Control Panel's scroll bar until CloseView's icon hoves into view (a hand clasping a magnifying glass), then click on it. With the CloseView Control Panel on screen (see Figure 33), you can switch the utility on and off, increase magnification, or invert the screen (ie white on black rather than the usual black on white), a function not accessible using keyboard shortcuts.

To quit CloseView completely, ridding the screen of the rectangular outline, retype Option-Command-O. Although the latter operation switches off the utility, it still uses valuable RAM memory – over 300K on a colour Mac – so if you are not going to use CloseView, de-install it by dragging it from the System Folder into another location (anywhere will do...) and restarting the Mac.

Chapter 8

WORKING WITH DISKS

Depending upon which model of Macintosh you have, it will be equipped with either one or two single-sided 3.5 inch floppy disk drives capable of storing 400K of applications and data, one or two double-sided 3.5 inch floppy disk drives capable of storing 800K of your data or a combination of internal floppy drives and an internal or external hard disk drive. The first Macs, the 128K and 512K machines, were equipped with a single 400K floppy drive which, because the Macintosh operating system makes such heavy demands upon backing storage, severely limited the efficiency of the machines. The introduction of the 512Ke Mac brought with it an internal 800K floppy drive. Every Mac thereafter incorporates a double-sided device (Classics, new SEs and onwards have a high density double-sided floppy drive known as the 'SuperDrive' capable of reading and writing 1.4Mb of data).

As stated previously, the Mac's System and Finder make extensive use of disk storage in order to provide the level of sophistication offered by the machine. Disks are never updated until absolutely necessary (such as when you're about to eject a modified, but not yet updated, disk, when launching an application, emptying the wastebasket and so on). This means that the Mac makes a considerable saving on time it would otherwise spend updating disks every time something changed. The result is a large increase in system efficiency and also explains why you cannot simply eject disks when whim decides as with other disk-based microcomputers.

Macintosh (and third party) hard disk drives can be internal, that is, fitted inside the Mac's case alongside the floppy drive, or external, that is fitted in their own housing, standing free of the Mac and connected via a cable and the Mac's SCSI (Small Computer Systems Interface pronounced 'Skuzzy') port. Internal drives are usually fitted to SEs, and IIs, external drives to the Mac 512Ke and Plus (very early Macs don't have a SCSI port and cannot be used with a hard drive without modification).

Although the addition of a hard drive to most computer systems is seen as rather a luxury, a hard drive on the Mac is an – almost – indispensible peripheral. You can use the Macintosh with a pair of floppy drives (a single floppy drive if you're exceptionally brave...), but you will find it hard to be productive or to achieve any worthwhile results without a hard drive. The Macintosh loads only the code which it needs into memory, swapping it for different code when some new function is required (similar to virtual memory – but not quite). If you are working with a machine equipped with floppies, there is a constant need to swap floppy disks in and out of drives in order to satisfy the demands of the Mac for code modules, System and Finder modules and so on. This really is an agonising and frustrating process which, with some software, appears to be endless.

Preparing floppy disks for use

Floppy disks come to you as blank discs of flexible plastic, coated with a magnetic substance similar to that covering the tape in domestic cassettes, and sealed inside an inflexible 'envelope' of hard plastic (note the spelling of 'disk' and 'disc'. The former is used to describe computer disks the latter, any other type of disc). Before you can use a floppy disk, its surface must be prepared by the Mac – a process known as 'initialising'. Magnetic 'ley-lines' are recorded onto the surface in order to divide it up into tracks and sectors, into and from which, the Mac can write and read data.

If your Mac is equipped with a single-sided disk drive, you can use double or single-sided floppies, but you will only be able to initialise one side of the disk. Single-sided disks provide 400K of storage space. If your Mac has a double-sided drive you can use double and single-sided floppies, formatting the former as double or single-sided (800K and 400K respectively) and the latter as single-sided only, providing 400K of space.

Initialising single-sided floppies

Insert the floppy disk into the Mac's internal disk drive metal end first and label uppermost. After a few moments, the Macintosh realises that the disk has not yet been initialised and a dialog will appear informing you of the fact and prompting you to go ahead with the process (see Figure 34). Click the One-sided button to format the disk as a single-sided, 400K floppy ('formatting' is another name for initialising). A warning dialog appears like that of Figure 35, to tell you that proceeding with the initialisation will remove all existing data from the disk. Click the Cancel button if you should decide not to go ahead, you will be returned to the Desktop. Click the Erase button and third dialog appears prompting you for a name for the new disk. It will be displaying the highlighted name 'Untitled'. If you want to name the disk, simply type over Untitled then click OK. If you click OK without naming the disk, it is given the name 'Untitled'.

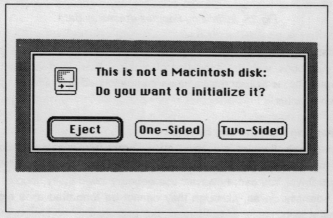

Fig 34. Initialising floppies

The Mac will now initialise the disk. A fourth dialog remains on screen throughout the process providing a progress report. If all goes well, you will be returned to the Desktop after initialising, and the new disk appears on the Desktop ready for use. If the initialising process could not be completed (because there is a fault with the disk for instance), then a dialog appears informing you of the fact. Clicking OK on this dialog ejects the faulty disk and returns you to the Desktop.

77

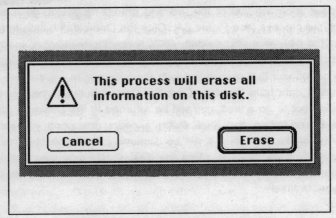

Fig 35. Initialising floppies erases all data

Initialising double-sided floppies

This process, with the exception of clicking 'Two-sided' instead of 'One-sided', is exactly the same as that described above for single-sided floppies.

Initialising high-density floppies

High-density floppies are physically different from single and double-sided disks and cannot be used in Macs not equipped with a SuperDrive. You can, however, use ordinary low-density floppies in high-density drives, although they cannot be formatted as a high-density disks.

Initialising high-density floppies is essentially the same as for single and double-sided floppies. The only exception is that the initialise dialog has only an Initialise button, there are no One-sided or Two-sided buttons.

Ejecting floppy disks

The Macintosh only updates a disk when absolutely necessary, such as when the wastebasket is emptied or an application is launched. This means however, that if you were to eject a disk before the Mac had had a chance to update it, valuable data could be lost or corrupted. In order to prevent you from ejecting disks willy-nilly, the Mac drive doesn't have an eject button. Instead, you must ask the Finder using one of several methods when you want to eject a disk. Finder decides whether the disk needs to be updated, performs the update if required, then spits out the disk.

The quickest method of ejecting disks is to drag them to the wastebasket. This doesn't delete the disk's data, but merely instructs the Finder to update then eject the disk (see Figure 36).

Alternatively, a disk can be ejected by clicking to highlight it, then selecting 'Eject' from the File menu (pressing Command-E has the same effect). Using the File menu Eject (and Command-E) method leaves a greyed-out image of the disk on the Desktop after ejection which can be removed by dragging it to the wastebasket.

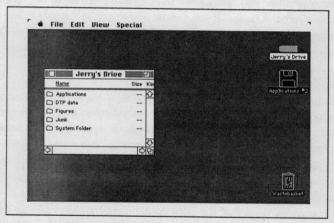

Fig 36. Ejecting a disk using the Trash

Another method of disk ejection is by typing Command-Shift-1 to eject the floppy in the internal drive and Command-Shift-2 to eject the floppy in the external drive. Both of these methods work from within applications as well as from the Desktop. As an alternative, when you want to eject a disk from within an application, select 'Open...' or 'Save As...' and when the file selector appears, choose a floppy to eject using the 'Drive' button, then click 'Eject'.

Deleting all of the data from a floppy disk

You cannot delete the data on a floppy disk by dragging its icon to the wastebasket, this will simply result in the disk being ejected (see above). To completely erase a floppy, double-click its icon to open a directory window, then press Command-A to select all of the files and folders. Now drag them to the wastebasket. Pull down the Special menu and select 'Empty Wastebasket'. The disk is erased. This method has the benefit of giving you a second chance. If you want to retrieve the files, don't empty the wastebasket, open it and drag out the files you want to save.

Alternatively, a disk can be erased in one action, by reinitialising it. Insert the disk into the Mac's internal drive, click on it to highlight it, then select 'Erase Disk' from the Special menu. A dialog appears asking whether you really want to completely erase all of the information from the floppy. If you should have second thoughts click the Cancel button or else click either One-sided or Two-sided. The drive is initialised to 400K or 800K respectively.

Backing up floppies

Although relatively robust, the floppy disk is nonetheless susceptible to electromagnetic radiation from televisions, telephones, computer monitors and so on. It is therefore wise to make backup copies of valuable disks, storing the originals in a safe place and to use the backup. The section entitled 'Copying one floppy disk to another' in Chapter 4, details several methods of backing-up floppy disks.

You can ensure that the data contained on a disk can't be overwritten by 'locking' the disk and there are two methods to do this. The first involves moving the plastic tab at the end of the disk opposite the sliding metal window, so that you can see through the hole. The disk is then physically 'write-protected' and cannot be written to without first covering the hole again using the sliding tab.

Alternatively, individual or groups of files on the disk can be locked using the Finder. Select the file you want to lock by clicking it. Pull down the File menu and select 'Get Info...' (or press Command-I). the Information dialog appears and you will see a

'Locked box' in its right-hand top corner. Click the Locked box to lock the object (a cross appears denoting lock status). Once locked, a file cannot be deleted from the disk.

Using a hard disk

Although the latest floppies can hold as much as 1.4Mb of data, if you are limited to a floppy-based Mac system, you will soon end up with piles of floppy disks. They're slow too, and modern, complex software requires many disk swaps during the course of a work session to produce anything worthwhile. Many applications, particularly the desktop publishing and image processing packages, only work with a hard drive. It is an inescapable fact of Mac ownership, that the only system to have is a hard drive-based system.

Fortunately, hard drives are not quite the financially remote devices they once were, and a small, say 20Mb hard drive, is within reach of all but the poorest Mac owner. Connect a hard drive to your Mac, and the latent power and sophistication of the System and Finder is released. No more disk swaps, no more heaps of floppies, just fast, efficient computing.

Hard drives have an enormous capacity – literally – to swallow files and it's with the hard drive, that the power of folders can really be appreciated. If all of your applications and documents were simply stored on the root directory of your hard drive, you would soon find it very difficult to locate anything. By using folders, one each for applications, one each for the documents they generate, others for utilities and so on, you can retrieve files easily and quickly and keep everything in order.

Care of your hard drive

Although robust in everyday use, a hard drive is nevertheless a delicate device, which must be treated with care in order to remain in peak condition. Follow these few tips to protect and get the most from your hard drive. Never move your hard drive (or Mac with internal hard drive), while the device is in operation. The disk(s) within a hard drive revolve at very high speeds and operate at much smaller tolerances than floppy disks. A sudden movement could cause the disk's read/write heads to come into contact with the surface of the spinning disk resulting in the loss of your data (and probably the complete destruction of the disk). Always switch off the drive and allow it to 'spin down' before moving it.

If you decide to switch the hard drive back on after switching it off, allow the drive to spin down before powering on. Switching on immediately can cause severe strain to the motor driving the device.

Never switch off your Mac's hard drive without first selecting 'Shut Down' from the Special menu. To do so, could result in lost data, because the Finder won't have time to update any modified files, close opened applications and so on.

Chapter 9

MULTIFINDER

Unlike mainframe and mini computers which have the ability to cope with many programs all running at the 'same' time, microcomputers are invariably limited to running just one application. The Mac's ability to access small utility programs in the form of Desktop accessories while running an application provides a kind of multi-tasking (as running more than one program at a time is known), but running two or more applications was impossible until, that is, Apple released MultiFinder.

MultiFinder is a version of the Finder which can manage several programs all running at once, allowing you to switch between them at will. MultiFinder also allows you to run 'background' programs such as print spoolers, which perform their functions while you continue to work with an application such as a word processor, spreadsheet or DTP package.

The advantages of using MultiFinder are endless. The multi-tasking Finder makes copying and pasting between different programs a very easy task. You can schedule other jobs to function automatically at convenient times of the day, back up your hard drive – a normally tedious process – while continuing to compute, return to the Desktop at any time in order to perform system-level functions such as renaming a disk, creating a new folder and so on. DAs work as normal when you are running MultiFinder, but they don't close automatically when you quit an application. This means that you can open a DA and use it, switch applications between whatever you were using when you selected the DA and a new program, then continue to use the DA. MultiFinder adds an incredible level of flexibility to an already powerful machine.

To use MultiFinder, you need to have version 5.0 or above of the system installed in your Mac. MultiFinder will work with all Macs from a Plus onwards with at least 1Mb of RAM memory. This however, is the absolute minimum. With only 1Mb of memory, you won't be able to run sophisticated software such as desktop publishing

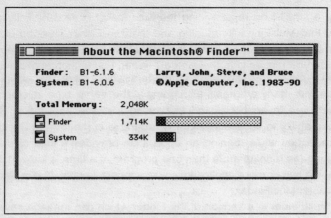

Fig 37. About the Finder...

packages, or, anything large or memory intensive in its operation (image manipulation programs are especially memory-hungry). 1Mb of RAM limits you to running only two or three very small programs such as archiving and disk utilities, early versions of the 'Mac' range of applications software and so on. To get the most from MultiFinder, your Mac should have 2Mb or more of RAM. (To determine the RAM quotient of your machine, pull down the Apple menu while on the Desktop and select 'About the Finder...'. See Figure 37.)

Running MultiFinder

MultiFinder is provided along with the Mac's system software. Before you use MultiFinder, make sure you have retrieved it from the Mac's system disks and stored it within the System Folder.

On the Desktop, pull down the Special menu and select Set Startup. A dialog appears enabling you to choose between running Finder and MultiFinder on startup (see Chapter 2, Figure 7). In the top half of the dialog click the MultiFinder button then click OK, you will be returned to the Desktop. Pull down the Special menu again and select Restart. When the Mac restarts, MultiFinder will be in control. Look at the top, right-hand corner of the menu bar, you'll see a small icon representing the Mac (see Figure 38). This tells you that MultiFinder is running and that the Finder Desktop is the current 'application' (the Desktop is treated just like any other application you run while in MultiFinder). When you launch applications, or move between them and the Finder Desktop, this icon changes, displaying the icon of whatever is current.

To launch an application, locate its icon and double-click as normal. The program will start and its icon will replace that of the Mac on the menu bar. If you want to return to the Desktop, don't quit the application, simply move to the icon on the menu bar and click it. The application is temporarily suspended, and the Finder Desktop appears (complete with its icon on the menu bar).

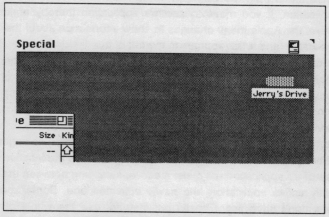

Fig 38. MultiFinder's menu bar icon

To launch another application, locate its icon and double-click. You can also launch several applications at once by clicking the first, shift-clicking (or lassoing...) the rest to select them all, then double-clicking any one. All will be launched. The multiple application launch only works with icons on the which have been dragged out onto the Desktop or with those which reside in the same window (because you can't shift-click or lasso files which are in different windows).

85

Moving around within MultiFinder

As well as being able to click the menu bar icons of applications to move between them, several other methods exist to achieve the same effect. The first involves the Apple menu. MultiFinder uses a modified version of the Apple menu which displays all currently open applications.

Switch on MultiFinder, then launch several applications. Now move to the Finder Desktop, and pull down the Apple menu. You will be presented with the usual array of DAs, but the bottom of the menu shows which applications are open and which is active (a tick appears to the left of the active application). The first option on the Apple menu (the About the Finder... option when you access the Apple menu from the Desktop) offers information about the active application. If you move to another application thereby making it active, the Apple menu changes to show information about the new application and a tick appears to the left of it.

You can move between applications by clicking them from the Apple menu and the effect is exactly the same as clicking on an application's icon on the menu bar.

Applications run in their own windows on the Finder Desktop. By shrinking the active application's window using the zoom box in the top, right-hand corner, you can see inactive windows belonging to other opened applications on the Desktop. Clicking the inactive window of an application will make it active, swapping between the currently active application and newly activated one. Some applications don't have zoom boxes but instead, use the whole display space to work in. If you are using an application of this type and you want to move to another application, use either the menu bar icon method or the Apple menu method.

Applications can also be activated by double-clicking their dimmed icons on the Desktop. If you open an application when running MultiFinder, a dimmed icon is displayed on the Desktop (in the same way that an open folder displays a window for itself and a dimmed icon in the window of the directory level in which the folder is stored). To move between applications using the dimmed icon method, return to the Desktop and double-click the dim icon.

Multiple startups

Just like the Finder, MultiFinder enables you to launch applications on startup. The difference is, of course, that MultiFinder allows you to launch several applications. You can then switch between them at will. This is extremely useful if you work regularly with a particular set of applications, they can be ready for you to work with automatically after starting up the Mac. Here's how to do it.

On the Desktop, select the applications you would like to launch at startup by clicking and shift-clicking or lassoing them (they must be in the same folder). Pull down the Special menu and select Set Startup. Click the Selected Items button in the Set Startup dialog. This action tells the Mac that the objects you clicked before entering the Set Startup dialog are the ones you would like to launch on startup. Click OK and you will be returned to the Desktop. Pull down the Special menu and select Restart. The Mac will restart and your chosen applications are launched.

Memory allocation and MultiFinder

Just like hard disk drives, memory used by MultiFinder can suffer from the problem of fragmentation. That is, although there may be enough RAM left to run an application, it is not in one contiguous block but rather, is broken up into small pieces which exist between other applications already loaded into memory.

For example, your Mac is equipped with 2Mb of RAM and after running the System, MultiFinder, and loading Application A (which requires 500K of RAM), there is 1Mb of contiguous memory space remaining. You then decide to load Application B which requires 600K of RAM. Fine. You now have Applications A and B installed in memory as well as the System and MultiFinder and 400K of RAM left over. Now you quit Application A. If you pull down the Apple menu and select About the Finder... to determine how much memory is left, you will be told 500K, i.e., the 500K freed by quitting Application A.

The reason is that 500K is the largest contiguous block of free RAM. Even though there is 900K free, it is broken into one block of 500K and one block of 400K divided by Application B in the middle.

You cannot run Application C which requires 700K even though there is enough memory available in the Mac, because MultiFinder cannot locate and piece together separate blocks of memory. The only solution is to quit Application B, thereby freeing all memory (except that occupied by the System and MultiFinder), then launch Applications B and C.

The way to avoid this problem is to try to ensure that you launch the applications you will most likely use longest, first. In that way, they are assigned to the lowest portions of available memory in one contiguous block. Applications which you intend to quit and restart are loaded later and occupy the other end of memory.

If, after running an application for a little while, you are told the application doesn't have enough memory in which to run correctly, try this. On the Desktop, select the the application's icon by clicking, then pull down the File menu and select Get Info... (or type Command-I). At the bottom of the Information dialog, there are two figures representing Suggested Memory Size and Application Memory Size. Click the Application Memory Size box to select it, then enlarge the figure contained within. This will force MultiFinder to assign more memory to the application when it's running.

Quitting MultiFinder

To turn off MultiFinder, pull down the Special menu and select Set Startup. Click the Finder button in the top half of the Set Startup dialog, then click OK. You will be returned to the Desktop. Now pull down the Special menu and select Restart. When the Mac restarts, MultiFinder has been switched off and Finder is in control.

To switch off MultiFinder temporarily, hold down Option when you start the Mac. This will have the effect of inhibiting MultiFinder and Finder will be in control. MultiFinder is still chosen however, and takes control next time you start the machine.

Choosing Shut Down from the Special menu when running MultiFinder results in a Save Changes...? dialog for those applications still open when you selected Shut Down. This feature makes it impossible to lose data by shutting down the Mac without saving, should you forget that you are running MultiFinder.

Chapter 10

THE FUTURE: SYSTEM 7.0

May 1989 saw the first preview of a System and Finder version that is as different from current versions, as the original was from the command line interpreters of the day. Although still very powerful and capable, Apple had decided that current System/Finder versions weren't appealing to corporate 'power' users as much perhaps, as the company would like. To this end, Apple instigated the development of System 7.0, a consistent and logical evolution of the current operating system and WIMP user interface.

Perhaps the most unusual feature of System 7.0, at least in microcomputer terms, is the use of virtual memory (VM). A concept widely used in the mainframe and minicomputer world, virtual memory is a method of simulating RAM memory using hard disks. The amount of 'memory' available to the computer is a sum of its RAM and a designated portion of the hard disk space. For example, a '12Mb' computer may have 2Mb of RAM installed and 10Mb of hard disk space allocated as memory.

VM works by breaking applications into 'pages' (i.e. fixed-size portions). When a particular part, or page, of the program is needed to perform a task, it is moved into RAM from disk (where the rest of the pages are stored). If another part of the program is needed, or the first part is no longer needed, it is moved back to the hard disk. Using the page technique, computers with limited RAM can be used with much larger and more complex applications requiring large memories.

The benefits of virtual memory are obvious. No longer is the computer user restricted to a machine with a small memory simply because RAM is too expensive to buy in large quantities. Backing storage in the form of hard drives is comparitively cheap and by using a large hard drive with a small amount of RAM, a very powerful machine indeed can be created.

In order to display fonts on screen, the Mac uses a method known as 'bitmapping'. This involves creating an 'image' of each character of a typeface using a series of 'bits' within the memory of the computer. Different point sizes within the same font all need to be seperately bitmapped, if the user is to avoid the jagged-edged, 'blocky' approximations of scaled up or down bitmapped fonts. System 7.0 purges the jagged-edged font for good, by providing outline fonts on screen.

Rather than using a bitmapped image of a font in order to display it, the outline of an outline font is described by a series of mathematical functions. Increasing the size of the font is a simple matter of feeding the functions with large numbers. The result is that fonts displayed on screen are very smooth and can be enlarged or reduced without degrading the quality.

There will be no need to use Font/DA Mover with System 7.0. Desktop accessories and fonts can be used simply by dragging them into the System Folder. This feature is one aspect in what is essentially, a blurring of the edges in the new system. Applications can be used just like DAs by installing and selecting them from the Apple menu, and DAs can be launched by double clicking their icons from the Desktop.

Using the new InterApplication Communications architecture, applications can be linked together so that they can swap data with ease. Users can define links so that updating the data in one application automatically updates the data in other, linked, applications. Applications can manipulate each other so that, for example, a word processor working with figures can access and manipulate a linked spreadsheet in order to recalculate the data.

Can I use System 7.0 with my Mac?
Almost certainly. System 7.0 will work with any Mac with at least 2Mb of RAM installed. Any Mac with a memory upgrade from a Plus onwards, will be able to make use of the new system. Certain parts of System 7.0 however, will not work without the appropriate hardware being available. Virtual memory requires a Paged Memory Management Unit (PMMU) to be installed. Motorola 68030-based Macs already have a PMMU, it's built into the processor. SEs and IIs (i.e., 68020-based machines), can have a PMMU installed. The

Mac Plus cannot be used with a PMMU and so cannot make use of the virtual memory feature provided by System 7.0. The low-end Macs can, however, enjoy many of the features provided by System 7.0 and the user must decide whether it is in his or her interests to upgrade.

Index

N.B. Page numbers in *italics* refer to illustrations

NOTES